Danger in the Comfort Zone

"A breakthrough! Bardwick shatters many of today's most cherished organizational principles and assumptions. She offers a viable new paradigm for those who choose to succeed in the new economy."

Don McQuaig
President, MICA Management Resources

"Dr. Bardwick challenges late 20th century corporate managers. . . . A stern but fair message, given today's competitive world."

Mal Watlington
Director, Organization Development &
   Compensation
Vickers, Inc.

"Bardwick tackles a complex, controversial subject and crystallizes it into readily understood principles. The Entitlement Habit threatens our personal lives and our nation. . . . This book should become 'must reading' for everyone interested in trying to deal with this epidemic problem."

Norman Schoenfeld
President, Elco Corporation

"We need new thinking on how to restructure our corporations. This book should be read by all executives."

Jack E. Bowsher
Retired IBM Director of Education
Author of *Educating America: Lessons Learned in the
   Nation's Corporations*

"A valuable book that adds a whole new dimension to our business analysis. It provides focus to those cloudy issues that surround our greatest resource— our people!"

Joe Ruffolo
President, North American Van Lines

"Bardwick has identified strategies for moving an organization from the pervasive modes of entitlement and fear to the most productive climate of earning through accountability. . . . Provides an innovative and valuable tool for managing change in corporate America."

Darrell T. Piersol
Director, Governor's Executive Development
   Program
University of Texas

Danger in the Comfort Zone

From Boardroom to
Mailroom—How to
Break the Entitlement
Habit That's Killing
American Business

Judith M. Bardwick

American Management Association

Library of Congress Cataloging-in-Publication Data

Bardwick, Judith M., 1933–
       *Danger in the comfort zone : from boardroom to mailroom—how to break
the entitlement habit that's killing American business / Judith M. Bardwick.*
           p.   cm.
       Includes bibliographical references and index.
       ISBN 0-8144-5059-8
       *1. Psychology, Industrial—United States.   2. Work—Psychological
aspects.   3. Entitlement attitudes—United States.   4. Employees—
United States—Attitudes.   5. Job security—United States.
6. Labor productivity—United States.   I. Title.*
HF5548.8.B243   1991
158.7—dc20   *91-19323*
                                                                          CIP

Printing number

10   9   8   7   6   5

This book is dedicated to
Rachel Elizabeth Ahearn
from her adoring grandmother.

Contents

Author's Note   *ix*

Acknowledgments   *xi*

Introduction: A New Look at a Familiar Problem   1

1 The American Dream Shattered   7

2 When Organizations Are Too Comfortable—The Lethargy of Entitlement   16

3 When Organizations Are Too Stressed—The Paralysis of Fear   31

4 When Organizations Are Revitalized—The Energy of Earning   48

5 Understanding How People Work—The Earning Curve   60

6 Moving Away From Entitlement—Increase Pressure   77

7 Moving Away From Fear—Decrease Pressure   95

8 Maintaining the Creative Energy of Earning   110

9 The New Paradigm   127

10 On the Personal Side   146

11 Questions and Answers   163

Notes on Sources   177

Index   *187*

Author's Note

Throughout this book I recount many stories of success and failure, of companies large and small, of people who feel energized by their work and those who feel terribly afraid.

Most of those that involve actual companies are taken from business periodicals and are so identified in each chapter's references (see pages 177ff.). In these cases, where names of companies and company leaders are given, they are the real names.

Stories not cited with a reference are the result of interviews I conducted with businesspeople in various industries. Quotations unattributed to a published source should be presumed to be from such interviews.

Still other stories are fictionalized accounts, inspired by real people with whom I am acquainted in one way or another but whose names are disguised.

Acknowledgments

I'd like to acknowledge the help given to me and express my thanks to the following special people:

To my literary agent, Barbara Hogensen of the Lucy Kroll Agency, for her marvelous competency.

To Adrienne Hickey, AMACOM's Senior Acquisitions Editor, for her piercing intelligence combined with powerful enthusiasm.

To my friends, venture capitalist Tom Murphy, and Norman Schoenfeld, President of Elco Corporation, who, early on, understood the theme and contributed wisdom and examples from their experience.

To Judy Taub of IBM in Poughkeepsie, who created the graphics as an unexpected and wonderful present.

To Bill Bryan, Program Manager; Tom Schappert, Manager, Management Development Programs; Ed Brewington, Director of Management Education, IBM Corporation, USA; and all at the IBM Management Development Center for their encouragement and commitment as the theme of this book has become part of the center's curriculum.

To the people at AMACOM, and my friends, Linda and Jack Finkelstein, Gary and Linda Eaton, Tom Murphy (again!), and Lee Doyle and Marita Sullivan, all of whom helped to create the title of the book.

To my daughter and first editor, Deborah Susan Bardwick, who thrilled me by clearly demonstrating greater writing skills than mine.

To free-lance editor Marty Stuckey of Portland, Oregon, who earlier edited *The Plateauing Trap,* and who created an even greater miracle with the manuscript of *this* book.

To my partner and husband, Captain Allen E. Armstrong, U.S. Coast Guard, Retired, who, more than anyone, contributes both indirectly and directly to all that I achieve.

To all of you, my heartfelt thanks!

Introduction

A New Look at a Familiar Problem

America no longer strides across the economic landscape as though she owned it. Our dominance is declining. We know it and we dislike it. All kinds of experts explain it: Politicians point to unfair trade practices, economists talk about the high cost of money, and engineers cite inefficient production techniques. But since this is a book by a psychologist, we're going to look at psychological causes.

Why is our productivity sagging? One reason rarely mentioned is that for many people the work ethic no longer shines as brightly as it used to. Too many Americans no longer work as hard or as well as they should. Even when people put in a lot of time, they don't accomplish much. They don't add value.

Employers unwittingly perpetuate this attitude by their failure to hold people accountable for doing good work. They don't really expect people to excel, so evaluating performance is a half-hearted exercise at best.

For the past twelve years I have spent most of my time as a consultant for some of the largest U.S. companies. As I observed the daily workings of more and more organizations, I found one consistent characteristic: Too many people put in "face time." They show up for work, and think that's good enough. Many even believe they're working hard. Most believe they're contributing.

For example, one company convened a committee of fifteen people from six different states to see how career plateauing—the lack of promotion opportunity—was affecting morale. I was asked to work with the group because I'd already given more than ten workshops on plateauing to its middle managers. In fact, half the committee members had been in those workshops.

"Our mission," the members told me, "is to find out how people feel about plateauing."

"But you already know," I protested. "You've been to the workshops yourselves. And you have heaps of survey data. It's your number one problem."

"We have to be sure," they said.

So the committee met for another year. Every six weeks or so, the members would leave their jobs and convene at headquarters to discuss a question they already had the answer to.

What's going on? U.S. corporations are run by some of the smartest people in the world. How could we have gotten to the point where workers are allowed to spend their time in such nonproductive ways? What has happened to our expectation that people should earn a real salary by doing real work? What happened to the Yankee notion that you ought to earn what you get?

This is what happened: The United States was so rich for so long that we no longer asked people to earn promotions, raises, and security. We stopped doing the work of requiring real work. As it turned out, we gave too much security to too many people. It wasn't good for our institutions and it wasn't good for our people. The dynamics we're talking about can be seen just as clearly in other relationships between people, especially in families.

Three years ago I was involved in a lengthy project for a major oil company. Over time, I developed friendships with several of the managers, including one middle manager in his forties. Even though his annual salary was somewhere around $50,000, he was always broke. A guilty divorced father, he spent about 40 percent of his income supporting his daughter. While the father was poor, the daughter was rich—private school, private tennis lessons, ritzy summer camp, and so forth.

One morning he pulled me aside, obviously upset, saying "I have to talk to you."

"Sure," I said. "What's up?"

"It's my daughter. I got a call from her last night."

"And?"

"And she said she called to remind me that I owe her a car."

"You *owe* her a car?"

"Yeah."

"Did she say *why* you owe her a car?"

"Because she's about to turn sixteen. She says I owe her a car because she's sixteen."

In that moment I "saw" the psychology of Entitlement.

What Is Entitlement?

Entitlement is the name I have given to an attitude, a way of looking at life. Those who have this attitude believe that they do not have to earn what they get. They come to believe that they get something because they are owed it, because they're *entitled* to it. They get what they want because of *who* they are, not because of what they *do*.

Entitlement is what I have been seeing in American corporations: people not really contributing, but still expecting to get their regular raise, their scheduled promotion. When this rich nation stopped requiring performance as a condition for keeping a job or getting a raise, it created a widespread attitude of Entitlement. Entitlement destroys motivation. It lowers productivity. In the long run it crushes self-esteem. And despite the layoffs of recent years, it is epidemic in this country. It's our legacy of the boom times that followed World War II.

The psychology of Entitlement is a concept. Using that concept, I have developed a very simple and very powerful model. In psychology, a model is a way of looking at relationships. The model is a lens, a tool to see familiar issues in a new way. It explains a lot of what is happening to us, and provides a clear perception of what we must do. My experience with using the model in business leads me to feel confident that it is a useful contribution in our drive for enhanced performance.

The Architecture of This Book

This book seeks to examine the collective body of American business, diagnosing unhealthy conditions and prescribing healthy alternatives. Its fundamental aim is to present a new perspective on the causes of our ailing productivity.

Chapter 1 sets the stage by briefly recounting economic trends since World War II and the attitudes that developed in our companies and among our workers during two main periods: the prosperous times just after the war and the downward cycle starting in the early 1970s.

Chapters 2 through 4 describe three psychological states and show what those states look like in organizations.

Entitlement: People are complacent; they get raises, bonuses, and benefits pretty much as a matter of course, so there is no incentive to work hard.

Fear: People are paralyzed; the threat of layoffs makes them focus on *protecting* their jobs rather than *doing* them.

Earning: People are energized by challenge; they know their work will be judged and that rewards will be based on accomplishment.

In these chapters we begin to see an inevitable progression. The economic environment of the larger marketplace creates a psychological environment in a particular organization that in turn controls people's attitudes toward their jobs.

Chapter 5 pulls the three psychological conditions together into one visual presentation called the Earning Curve. This graphic makes clear the dynamic flow from one condition to another, and shows the relationship between psychological state and productivity level. When put into the form of a graph, the idea becomes stunningly simple.

Chapters 6 through 8 help senior executives and managers develop a strategy for improving productivity by changing the psychological environment of their companies, thus moving from the lethargy of Entitlement or the paralysis of Fear to the vigor of Earning. Chapter 9 coalesces the strategies into a description of the dynamics of change and focuses the spotlight on key features of the new paradigm.

Most of this book will be directed toward business, but the model that will unfold has many applications. In Chapter 10, we look at the psychology of Entitlement from a personal level. Entitlement is at its core a very simple idea, but its very simplicity begets lots of questions. Chapter 11 is a collection of the questions I am most commonly asked when I present seminars and workshops on Entitlement issues in organizations.

The Task Ahead

Historically, rich organizations in a rich nation were willing to be "nice" and carry even those who didn't add value. In large bureaucracies, it was also easy to hide, which made it even more likely that people would not be held accountable for real work. Over time, everyone who is not held accountable has all the time in the world.

In organizations where there is no sense of urgency, morale and motivation are usually very low. There's no vitality, no energy. And what of the people who work in those organizations? At first, such total security seems wonderful. But before long, a kind of heavy complacency settles in. When the system is unresponsive, when the organization does not require work that makes a difference, when outstanding performers are not rewarded for their accomplishments, and when underachieving performers are not punished, people become apathetic. In organizations where nothing much happens regardless of whether you do something exceptional or just show up in the morning, the best people lose heart and motivation is reduced near the lowest common denominator.

The task that faces this nation is a move from a psychology of Entitlement to one of Earning. But that will take great courage, because leaving Entitlement requires a sojourn into the psychology of Fear. Holding the flashlight for that journey— leading the way from Entitlement through Fear to Earning—is the goal of this book.

1

The American Dream Shattered

Generation after generation of Americans have climbed up the economic ladder, each standing higher than the one before it. The American Dream is based on a contract that says, "If you work hard, you are going to be more successful than your parents were." Those born in the Depression years found themselves, after the war, with opportunities and resources their parents had never imagined. Their children, the baby boomers, grew up with even higher expectations of success.

The same economic trends that realized that dream for an extraordinary number of people also spawned a certain way of thinking. In American companies, an attitude of Entitlement developed in both the organizations themselves and among the people who worked in them. What happened to the dream, and what happened to that way of thinking, is the focus of this chapter.

America the Prosperous

The years after World War II offered more people the opportunity for success than ever before in the United States. The boom years lasted approximately from the end of the war in 1946 to the recession and oil embargo of 1973 (the exact dates vary for different industries and organizations). The fat times were created by four extraordinary conditions that occurred simultaneously.

The first was the growth rate of the economy. For more than twenty-five years, despite several recessions, the U.S. economy sustained its highest growth rate ever. After sixteen years of depression and war, we experienced an explosive growth in consumer demand.

The second was our dominance in the world economy. During all those years, we were simply the unquestioned leader.

The third variable was the incredibly high birth rate that began in 1946. In the eighteen years from 1946 to 1964, 76 million babies were born.

In combination with the high growth rate of the economy, the high birth rate created the fourth condition: the tremendous expansion in the size of companies and organizations. In the decades that followed the war, institutions grew at the highest rates the United States ever experienced. In some companies, like AT&T, middle management grew by 500 percent. The 1950s and 1960s have been called "the Golden Age of the U.S. corporation."

Together, these four extraordinary conditions created unparalleled opportunities. And the people who could take advantage of those opportunities had been born in the 1920s and 1930s when the birth rate was the lowest in U.S. history. Thus, people who grew up during the Depression went to work at a time when the opportunity rate was at its highest.

Entitlement: The Legacy of Prosperity

On the surface, unlimited growth would seem to be a good thing. Companies are strong and profitable and people have no trouble finding good jobs, so everyone is secure and happy. But it is one of the premises of this book that it is possible to have too much of a good thing, that those years of prosperity have now backfired. Gradually, insidiously, prosperity created the crippling condition called Entitlement, where workers have no real incentive to achieve and managers have stopped doing the work of requiring real work. (The dynamics of Entitlement are discussed in Chapter 3.)

How did this happen? For most of its history, the United

States has honored a tradition of self-sufficiency; individuals have been expected to take care of themselves and to earn their way. But by the 1950s, we had become a nation that expected our society to provide for its citizens and we expected U.S. companies to take care of their employees. What changed?

The answer has both an economic and a psychological component. Economically, Entitlement comes from two forces at work in those incredible years after World War II: economic boom and demographic bust. With a limited pool of employees, rich organizations kept all their workers, no matter how well or how poorly they performed. In spite of this, business and industry flourished. Entitlement is a legacy of these years of affluence.

At that time, too, the social sciences gained new significance in the popular culture and there was a shift in our beliefs about behavior. Psychology, psychiatry, and sociology all try to analyze and explain why people behave as they do. As we focused on the reasons for incompetence or·nonperformance, we ceased judging. When people's work falls off in the midst of a nasty divorce, for example, we hesitate before we burden them with criticism. It's very difficult to be judgmental when you understand the cause.

As a nation we came to a new understanding of human behavior, one that led us to tolerate low achievement while also enjoying a tremendous economic prosperity. We were so rich we could afford to be kind.

Under the double influence of their corporate compassion and their rich treasuries, in the postwar decades organizations began to grant job security without regard to how well people worked and how much they contributed. They stopped evaluating employees and discharging those who were nonproductive; they failed to hold people accountable for their performance.

This tolerance of nonperformance was especially obvious in the case of plateaued employees, those who had reached the upper limit of their promotability. They were not required to be productive; they were not dismissed for being unproductive. Instead, plateaued people were allowed to hang around, read the paper, and serve on insignificant committees, such as the

Christmas Party Committee, the Annual Picnic Committee, the Committee to Allocate Office Space.

There was an unarticulated agreement that plateaued people gave up the excitement of being in the mainstream of the business in return for the comfort and security of lying on the shelf until it was okay to retire. Thus, management no longer did the work of evaluating their performance.

Over time, that attitude originally directed toward plateaued workers spread to all employees. Organizations no longer expected to get performance from every employee all the time. In the affluent years, companies were doing so well they could afford to carry nonproductive people.

Despite the recent and ongoing ravages of downsizing, that trend continues today in many companies, boosted by changes in the law. Under the old common-law concept of employment at will, the company had all the power; managers could fire laggards on the spot. Today it is very difficult to fire someone without running the risk of legal counteraction. When organizations don't fire, they never get rid of unproductive people. They can't afford to have them in responsible positions, so they make up jobs for them where they can't do any harm. Therefore, organizations end up with lots of employees who don't produce and who keep their jobs just by showing up. If the organization is really fat, these people even get merit raises. It is this corporate tolerance for nonperformance that has generated the psychology of Entitlement in American companies.

The End of the Dream

By the 1950s and 1960s, our economic lead was so total it was inconceivable that it could change. But in the early 1970s, our seemingly invincible strength was hit with a series of economic blows: the recession and oil embargo of 1973; the inflation and stagflation that followed; the recession of 1979; the recession of 1981–1982; and the stock market crash of October 18, 1987, Black Friday, when the Dow fell more than 500 points. In less than a generation, our nation went from feeling confident to feeling threatened.

The sons and daughters who assumed the American Dream from their parents are finding that for them the dream has begun to unravel. Hard work no longer guarantees upward mobility. No one anticipated what Paula Rayman of Wellesley calls "the middle-class squeeze—falling behind while getting ahead." As a group, the baby boomers are actually downwardly mobile. They're not able to live as well as adults as they did as kids. Richard Michel, an economist at the Urban Institute in Washington, D.C., says "The young middle class has experienced a dramatic decline in its ability to pursue the conventional American dream: a home, financial security, and education for their children." Lately, the average American has been running hard to stay in place.

The History of the New Business Reality

Something very fundamental has changed in economic realities. Productivity, which was growing at 4 percent a year, is now little more than 2 percent and is not rising. In February 1990, *Business Week* reported:

> Productivity in the U.S. has been in the doldrums for a long time—but now, its poor performance poses a threat to the economy. Output per hour in nonfarm industry rose at a paltry 1.2% annual rate in the 1980s—no improvement from the 1970s. Moreover, productivity heads into the 1990s at its slowest pace since the 1981–82 recession.
>
> For the coming year, poor productivity growth has a number of implications for the outlook—all bad.

We are the largest debtor nation in the world. The number of positions in our large corporations—white collar and blue collar—is declining. Previously immune to foreign competition, we are now unceasingly aware of it. Nations of the Pacific rim and Europe are lining up, competing for our markets, wooing our customers.

What this situation means for American companies is that

they can no longer afford to perpetuate conditions of Entitlement. What it means for American workers is that companies
can no longer afford to carry entitled, nonproductive people.

Why is it really necessary to get high levels of productivity
from everyone? One of the key answers is the shift to a global
economy. A global economy is one in which you no longer have
your customers. Competitors can come from your own country,
a neighboring country, or a country on the other side of the
world in search of your customers.

With air travel there is no distance, there is only time. And
sometimes there is no time. Communication by phone and fax
is instantaneous. You can talk anywhere and deal anywhere instantly. And so can your competitors. In combination with increasing deregulation, the immediate result of this technology
is that you have to fight for, service, and please your customers,
because they literally have all the choice in the world. In the
end, the only one who can provide job security is the customer.

Drew Lewis, chairman of Union Pacific, is trying to get the
railroad to be more responsive to customers. In a recent meeting, several hundred rail workers demanded guaranteed jobs.
He told them, "If I promise you a lifetime job, what is that
worth if we're not competitive? It's worth a deck chair on the
Titanic."

When the customer is the only source of security, then security has to be continuously earned. Therefore, in a fundamental way, organizations cannot promise security because they
don't have it. Organizations have to earn security through performance. And so they must demand performance from their
employees, those individuals who make up the organization. No
organization can afford to carry unproductive people anymore.
Cost cutting has dominated the defensive strategies of corporate survival in recent years. Stripping away euphemisms like
downsizing and *reduction in force,* the reality is one of layoffs, even
of productive people. Job security for many is gone or at risk.

Beginning in the early 1980s, even corporations that had
never fired people began to do so. One estimate is that in the
1980s more than 1 million managers and professionals were cut
from the corporate ranks. Another estimate is that the number
may be as high as 2 million.

Later in the decade the rate of cuts increased, and 1989

and 1990 saw more cutbacks than ever. The actual numbers vary according to who's counting and how middle manager and white collar are defined, but one fairly recent count emphasizes the accelerating problem: 111,285 middle managers and executives lost their jobs in all of 1989; in the first quarter of 1990 alone, the number was 110,152. In 1990, announcements of corporate cuts occurred at twice the 1989 rate. This retrenchment is cutting deeply in the ranks of middle and top-level managers and is now occurring in a wide range of companies that had not been affected in the 1980s.

Even organizations like Eastman Kodak, Polaroid, Exxon, AT&T, and Xerox, which have always had policies that amounted to lifetime employment, have begun to push out people through early retirement and firings. Eastman Kodak did away with 10 percent of its work force when it cut 13,000 positions. Exxon reduced its staff at headquarters in New York from 1,400 to 320. Hewlett-Packard offered early retirement packages to 1,800 employees. By the beginning of 1988, General Motors had cut its white-collar labor force by 25 percent and announced a further cut of 25,000 for 1989. Xerox pared down by 20 percent in the 1980s and said another one-third of its management and administrative staffs would be cut in the early 1990s.

The private sector is not alone in the changes it faces. By 1983, it had become clear that the employment boom in the public sector was also hard hit and had become an employment bust. In the middle of 1980, the federal government employed 16,735,000 people. Two and a half years later, after the recession of 1981–82, it was down to 15,197,000. In many local and state governments the declines have continued, some dramatically. During the recession, for example, the state of Michigan cut its 70,000 employees by 10,000.

One thing that made all the costs especially hard to bear was that after we recovered from the recession of 1981–82, the rate of cuts increased. Major cuts took place in the mid-1980s, when employment was high, interest rates were low, there was little inflation, the stock market was strong, and the economy was growing. This situation increased people's sense of vulnerability.

What makes the changes even more difficult is they are

likely to be permanent. According to Robert Tomasko, nine significant trends created the accelerated rate of downsizing, despite the strength of our economy. In addition to the trends we have already discussed, the movement of many American companies overseas, where costs are lower, has contributed. Sharply falling energy and commodity prices, most clearly in oil, have required industry cost-cutting in the producing industries. Many industries that were formerly regulated are now deregulated. After initial growth phases, deregulated industries now face tremendous competition and competitive price cutting. They, too, need to cut overhead. We've seen an enormous number of mergers and acquisitions. And, lastly, if we follow Britain's footsteps and privatize some of our government functions,* we can predict also the loss of public jobs as the businesses cut costs in pursuit of profits.

All the factors that Tomasko has identified have very little to do with short-term business cycles. The implication is that the times have truly changed and the changes are permanent.

The Changing Employment Contract

The contract of understanding and obligation between employers and employees has changed. Most of our organizations, but especially those that enjoyed decades of Entitlement, maintained a powerful and implicit contract with their employees. In exchange for unswerving loyalty and a level of commitment that entailed putting the company before family or self, you had a position for life. The company invested in you and took care of you and gave you a raise every year. You could count on it.

The contract is particularly important for middle managers. Traditionally, blue-collar workers were protected by their unions, but middle managers were protected by a strongly felt and very specific invisible contract that said:

> Take care of business and we'll take care of you. You
> don't have to be a star; just be faithful, obedient, and

---

*The United States Office of Personnel Management has proposed that many of its 600,000 jobs, ranging from data processing to vehicle maintenance, be spun off into businesses.

only modestly competent, and this will be your home as long as you want to stay. We may have to lay off blue-collar workers now and then, or even cut off some heads at the very top, but unless we are in the deepest kind of trouble you will remain on the payroll. You are Family.

The old contract developed when national economic growth was great and the working population was relatively small. Not only could organizations afford to develop long-range plans for their employees but it was in their best interests to do so. Organizations offered promotion and other work-related benefits as well as life insurance, pensions, wellness, recreation, and social programs. Along with these benefits came the implicit understanding that the employee would remain with the organization and that the organization would not fire or lay off the employee.

In the new contract, the organization no longer assumes that it will employ people for the whole of their career. Therefore, it is unwilling to take care of them. Instead of being taken care of, employees are increasingly expected to become self-managing. There will be less long-term development of skills and more buying of them. People will be valued more for present performance and less for historic loyalty.

Increasingly, organizations will ask of potential employees, What do you bring to the table now? What skills do you have that are a contribution now? As a result, organizations will compete in the recruitment of outstanding people not just at the entry level but at every level. Similarly, people will compete with each other for employment, not just at the beginning but over the whole course of their careers.

The United States is not the same place it was after World War II. Our economy is no longer bursting at the seams with exuberant growth. We have lost the psychological sense of being in the driver's seat. We can no longer presume our dominance or our wealth. Individuals are learning they may not be able to afford something, like a house, that they assumed they would have as a birthright. And the nation is learning that it, too, cannot afford everything.

2

When Organizations Are Too Comfortable — The Lethargy of Entitlement

In 1983, I received a call from a human resources executive in a major manufacturing corporation, a Fortune 100 company. The company had a reputation for never firing anyone; children followed their parents into the company. The executive who called said the company was concerned about the low numbers of women and minorities in management and asked me to design a one-day workshop that would examine the psychological issues underlying the numbers.

A committee of four people had already spent about a year on the project, reading, interviewing, observing, and meeting with consultants nationwide. After developing a workshop outline, I met with the committee members for a day and explained my recommendations for the workshop.

Several weeks later, I was asked to return for five more days to go over the workshop design in detail. The entire five-day discussion was tape recorded and a secretary spent weeks transcribing every word for later study. Still, the committee didn't compare my suggestions with those of other experts it had consulted and it made no suggestions for change.

A month and a half later I was asked back. The committee had hired someone to be in charge of the workshop and thought it would be a good idea to bring him up to speed. Even though everyone had access to the transcriptions of our earlier discussions, we spent a week going through the same material again.

Two months later, I received another call. The committee had decided to go forward with the workshop, but it wanted handouts. Could I return for a week to write an outline?

Three months after that, we did a week of pilot workshops. During this entire period there had not been a single modification to my original workshop design. Each day, all five members of the committee sat at the back of the room and wrote down everything that was said. They also collected evaluations from every participant, which were very high. They were very busy, but they didn't say anything and they didn't change anything. Nothing happened as a result of their work.

Months later, I was asked to return for more pilot workshops. Those same five people sat in the back of the room and took notes all day. Again, they collected evaluations. Again, the evaluations were very high. And that was the end of the project. The actual workshop never occurred.

The committee members had put two years into planning the event. Once we reached the point of *doing* something (instead of planning) they simply stopped working on it. Neither they nor anyone in higher management seemed to care about the enormous investment in developing a program that never took place. It was as if the task were to design a workshop; no one seemed to remember that the real task was to prepare more minority workers and women for management positions.

I felt as though I had fallen into Alice's rabbit hole and landed in a strange land. Everyone but me had known all along that we had been engaged in a conspiracy of play acting. They were playing at working. If you define working as achieving something, they were not working. They were busy looking busy. And the organization, because it did not say "That won't do," was in effect saying "That's fine."

This company is a classic case of an organization stuck in the state of Entitlement. Over the years, the company has grown accustomed to mediocre performance levels. Mediocre has become normal so that even today those five committee members and their bosses see nothing remarkable in having spent two years planning a one-day workshop that never happened. This phenomenal waste of time will not jeopardize any-one's job security.

Entitlement in American Organizations

"This company is just like one big family." Chances are, when-ever you hear people say that, they're talking about a company that is stuck in Entitlement. They're commenting on the warm sense of belonging, but unconsciously they're also talking about not having to earn their place. In the family at work, as in the family at home, Entitlement means you belong and you benefit precisely because you belong.

Expressed simply, Entitlement is the result of too much generosity. We give people what they expect and we don't hold them accountable for meeting criteria of excellence. In business it commonly happens because managers are unwilling to do the work of requiring work. Frequently it's because they want to avoid discord and bad feelings. Very often it arises from pity: We don't hold people accountable for results because we don't think they can perform. Good performance, poor perform-ance, or no performance are all treated the same. In the work-place, people feel entitled when they have so much security that they don't have to earn their rewards.

- They keep their jobs and collect their regular paychecks no matter whether they produce much or little.
- They get their annual raises regardless of their contri-bution during the year.
- They are promoted because they have the right amount of seniority, not because they have demonstrated their superior competence for the higher-level jobs.
- They receive a year-end bonus because it's the end of the year, not because they've made notable achievements.

When people don't have to earn what they get, they soon take for granted what they receive. The real irony is that they're not grateful for what they get. Instead, they want more. It is the terrible cycle of Entitlement.

It is inaccurate to think of these issues only in terms of lower-level workers. Entitlement often goes through the highest ranks to the executive level. That's what we see when large corporations (General Motors was one) freeze wages, lay workers off, and give executives big bonuses. The same thing happened in some of the savings and loans that were taken over by federal administrators: They were losing money like crazy, but they were giving top officers hefty bonuses. Too often, there are no market forces operating at the highest level—executives get perks and bonuses irrespective of company performance—so the company operates to primarily benefit those who run it.

Too Much Security

"I've worked here a long time and have done what you expected. I've earned my security." That is the working presumption of the majority of people who work in our various government bodies, in all levels of our schools, in our large and powerful unions, and in our mature and prosperous corporations. It amounts to total job security. Too much security is what Entitlement is all about.

Job Security

Some groups of people (schoolteachers, for example) have formal tenure. They set a precedent for others to successfully argue their right to have the same certainty. In recent years those precedents became transformed into court decisions so that it became legally difficult to fire employees.

Under the old common-law concept of employment at will, the company had all the power; managers could fire laggards on the spot. Today it is very difficult to fire someone without running the risk of legal counteraction. As of January 1989, courts in forty-six states have issued rulings that erode the doctrine of employment at will, and at least thirteen states now recognize a vague principle known as the covenant of good faith and fair dealing, which says that each judge is free to decide whether or not an employee was fired without adequate cause.

Employers cannot fire employees without reasonable cause—for example, a reduction in force, unauthorized absenteeism, misbehavior, or failure to perform. For lawyers, this is proving to be a major windfall: a typical wrongful discharge suit in California, for example, awards damages of $700,000 if the employer loses.

With legal restrictions on top of tenure systems on top of a longstanding culture of nonaccountability, entitled organizations find it practically impossible to get rid of a nonproductive employee, even if they were so inclined. Often acutely ineffective people aren't fired; they are praised and passed on to someone else.

Too much security first shows up in organizations in the evaluation system. Where job security is absolute, companies gradually become less and less rigorous in their performance evaluation. Especially when people have reached their career plateaus, distinguishing between them becomes less important. Wherever it's very hard to fire people, evaluations are useful only to identify people who should be promoted. They are irrelevant for identifying those who should be penalized, because firing, which is the truly significant punishment, is no longer available. Thus, even though the formal culture may say "Evaluate!" the operating culture says "Why bother?"

Then, security generalizes to other aspects of life in the organization. First there is total job security; then seeking security, playing it safe in all dimensions, takes over as the dominant mode of operation.

When Security Is Institutionalized

Over time, the organization's culture becomes an accumulation of hundreds of ways to achieve security and avoid mistakes. These means are informal at first, then formal, until eventually Entitlement is fully institutionalized. This is the truly insidious danger with Entitlement: It settles in everywhere, and becomes part of the mortar that holds the organization together. Here are some of the ways that entitled organizations institutionalize security:

- Informal tenure for everyone
- An appraisal system that has no real impact
- A promotion system that doesn't reflect individual merit
- An emphasis on precedent
- Lots and lots of rules
- Lots and lots of paper
- A compensation system that doesn't really reflect what people do
- Committees with no real authority
- Rewards for fine-tuners, and punishment for innovators
- A formal hierarchy in which differences in power dictate permissible behavior
- Talk about pushing power down without real empowerment or delegation
- Layers of people whose jobs are making sure no mistakes are being made

Rules, Bureaucracy, and Hierarchy

From a culture made up of informal ways to avoid risk, it's a very easy step to a formalized system of precise rules, regulations, and procedures telling people exactly what to do so they don't make a mistake. When confidence is low, people are more comfortable if they know the boundaries of what's okay and what's not. Rules exist to tell people what they cannot do.

In the 1950s and 1960s, there were far fewer rules than there are now. As Entitlement became more common, the number of rules increased. The Defense Department controls its 134,000 employees through 4,000 laws and 30,000 pages of regulations. The department's acquisition regulations take 1.2 million lines or enough to fill 600 books that are 300 pages long: There are 20 pages for Defense Department fruit cake, 15 pages for T-shirts, and 7 pages for pencils.

The old AT&T provided rules for every contingency. The manual of *Bell Systems Instructions* took up 24 feet of shelf space, and the *Operating Procedures* manual took a few dozen feet more. One section alone—"How to Properly Take an Order"—was more than 1,200 pages long!

Before long, rules come to have a life of their own. Knowing and following the regulations becomes the end in itself. The emphasis is more on how things are done and less on what is accomplished. People become preoccupied with "doing it right," which comes to mean "by the book." It becomes more important than "doing it best."

Organizations with lots of rules usually have lots of checkers to make sure the rules are being obeyed. Institutions with too much security thus tend to become more and more bureaucratic. They add layers of rules to ensure that mistakes are never made, and layers of people to ensure that the rules are explained, understood, updated, and followed.

Prior to 1981, General Electric was a prime example of a bureaucracy. In the area of finance there was an unceasing need for longer, more detailed financial reports. One business unit put out seven daily reports, one of which made a pile 12 feet high, with sales data on every product manufactured— hundreds of thousands of items. When Jack Welch took over as CEO (chief executive officer) of GE in April 1981, the focus on bureaucracy changed. Welch considers bureaucracy "evil," believing it threatens productivity because it encourages people to look at the company and its procedures rather than at customers and the competition. He says "This internal focus has wasted our time, wasted our energy, frustrated us, made us so mad some nights over some bureaucratic jackass boss that we'd punch a hole in the wall."

As they add layers, bureaucratic organizations tend to become increasingly hierarchical. Then the culture, too, becomes ever more hierarchical; people pay a lot of attention to the differences in power at the different rungs on the ladder. Psychologically, the ladder is very tall. Where hierarchical status is really important, power is distributed from the top down.

The Consequences of Top-Down Power

In this kind of atmosphere, what happens to the employees? What does this kind of environment do to people's attitude about themselves, about their bosses, and about their work?

Pseudowork

In entitled organizations people concentrate on what looks good. *Looking* good is more important than *doing* good. Over time, form supplants substance. The appearance of being busy is equal in value to actually achieving. Doing excellent staff work, writing reports, doing analyses, creating committees, and holding meetings are more important than competing successfully in the marketplace. People lose sight of what's important; they are rewarded for simply putting in time.

Entitled organizations create red tape, paperwork, and pseudowork. There are endless meetings where nothing happens and there is no follow-up. Thousands of hours are invested in writing reports that no one reads. People write ponderous memos "to the file," explaining why they took no action.

A friend of mine who is a ranking officer in the State Department tells the story of interviewing a civil servant who wanted to transfer from Washington to Paris.

"Tell me what you do," my friend asked.

"I write reports."

"No, tell me what you accomplish. What will the result of your work be?"

"That's a very upsetting question."

Passivity

In hierarchical organizations, where power comes from the top down, people look up and wait for orders. They pay close attention to the nuances of behavior from those with more power. They know there is an unwritten contract that says "If you behave, you'll be okay." No wonder people pay so much attention to knowing the rules, following the boss's lead, knowing the right people, never making errors rather than risking, trying, and innovating.

I am distressed at how passive these hierarchical organizations make people. Even though they may appear active, they are waiting. More than anything, they keep their eye on the boss, waiting to be told what to do.

I remember going to a meeting with the CEO of a Baby

Bell and his top aides. I'd been doing some work in the company and they wanted to hear my impressions. The CEO is a smart and jovial man. He welcomed me with huge gestures of enthusiasm to his enormous boardroom table. Despite the hugging welcome, I sat alone at one end and he sat a football field away at the other end. His top people sat at his end, but not anywhere near his chair. The people who had brought me into the organization were not in the topmost group. They sat away from the table, flat against the wall.

"Judy," the CEO said, "I want you to tell me the truth. Tell me what you saw. Don't hold anything back!"

"Sure," I said. "Of course."

He leaned back. I started to talk. He interrupted. We listened to him. His aides elaborated on what he said. We all looked at him. He talked again. We continued looking at him. I tried to interject. He kept on talking. We kept on looking at him. He kept on talking. After thirty minutes I interrupted. "You asked me to tell you what I've seen. If you want me to tell you, you have to let me talk."

The room got dead quiet. No one looked at me. Everyone looked at the CEO. He made up his mind. He laughed. He said, "Okay. You're right. I'll shut up."

In that psychologically hierarchical organization, the CEO thought he was a democratic leader, a person who practiced participative management, who went out of his way to invite input from others. But the culture was so pervasively hierarchical, his right to be the authority was so ingrained, that it wasn't possible for him to notice that he always told and never listened. Formal or hierarchical authority is so basic to that institution that attempts to empower people and get them to be initiating must remain impotent and superficial until the culture is thoroughly transformed.

In bureaucratic, hierarchical organizations, nobody makes waves. I call them Country Club places. No one disagrees with anyone else in a substantive way. Asked an opinion, they'll check with the boss, swiftly agree, or hide through cliches. Questions are discouraged and giving answers is avoided. No one contradicts a position already taken. People avoid conflict and accountability by not talking to each other. Instead, they slide past each other. Discussion really means waiting for the boss to say what's right.

In one organization with which I am familiar this is carried to an extreme: At meetings, people who are supposed to give a report stand up and say their piece. Then the boss asks for comments. Someone always says "That was very interesting." Then the boss nods, thoughtfully, and thanks the first person for the report. Then the next person stands and delivers a report, which is always "interesting." Then that person is thanked. It's very common for people to repeat the last sentence or two of what was just said and nod their heads up and down, up and down, as though they were really thinking.

People in those kinds of organizations are like a long line of penguins. They're dressed for success. But while their feet point forward and they use words like *Initiate! Confront! Lead! Innovate!*, the truth is that they waddle from side to side. While their heads face forward, their eyes gaze skyward, toward those higher on the ladder. They're cautious and passive. Dependent and feeling vulnerable, they're endlessly looking for recognition, preoccupied with how they're doing.

Resentment and Ambivalence

In hierarchical organizations, there is basically very little real respect for people who are at the lower levels. Top-down, paternalistic organizations really do run in ways that express the belief that employees are not capable. Management tells subordinates the rules and subordinates learn them. The rules themselves say "I don't trust your judgment." Is it any wonder morale is poor?

Surveys in these organizations find employees very angry. They're saying "You don't show respect for us as individuals. You don't give me increasing responsibilities. You don't let me make decisions. You treat me like a child. You keep telling me what to do. You never ask me. You never listen to me. Besides that, you don't punish people who do nothing. I'm working my head off and you let those jerks get away with it. I end up having to do their work as well as my own. Why am I knocking myself out?"

But even as they resent being treated like children, being given rules to follow, people are also ambivalent. Rules give us an easy way to master situations. Rules give us security and protect us from having to think and make judgments.

Dependence itself makes people ambivalent. Even though dependent people lean on the hierarchy to sustain and support them, they don't like being powerless. They want the support yet bitterly resent the fact that they need it. People resent the presumption of incompetence that underlies dependence. But without confidence, they remain dependent and more resentful than grateful.

This situation may partly explain why entitled people so often become greedy. In addition to grabbing for security, boxed into resenting what they get, they unconsciously also seek to get even by demanding even more.

Greed

In these organizations managers talk about what "I do for my people" and employees ask "What will you do for me?" Nowhere do we hear people say what they plan to do for themselves. Entitlement creates people who keep asking what else is going to be done for them. And what is done is never enough.

Arnold Jones, for example, spent most of his career with a large manufacturing company that has always taken pride in how it deals withs its employees. He recently ran into Peter, a man from another division of the same company. They hadn't seen each other for a couple of years.

"What's happening?" Arnold asked.

"That damn company," Peter said. "First they force me to move from Stamford to Los Angeles. I hate Los Angeles, and so does my wife. I had to sell the house and pull the kids out of school. Then, less than a year later, they pull me back to Connecticut, for god's sake."

Peter happened to leave out one small detail: He'd gone to California as an executive in a division that lost $100 million during his tenure. He could have said "We really screwed up. We lost a bundle. I'm really grateful I've still got a job. I'm going to give this one everything I've got." Instead, he said, "They jerked me around one more time. Damn them."

In 1989, a manager at IBM told me the company had just announced lower earnings, a buy-back of its stock, and a plan to cut costs by getting 10,000 people to take early retirement. In this belt-tightening atmosphere, an employee asked for an "open door," IBM's term for an employee complaint of unfair treatment; these complaints can be directed as high in the organization as the employee wants, all the way to the chairperson. "Imagine," this manager said, "this open door was brought by a guy with a high school education. He's a technician and he must be pretty good because he earns almost $90,000 a year. You know what he was complaining about? Getting a 6 percent raise! He said he was entitled to 11 percent because that's what he always got."

Another example of greed is illustrated by Sam Gershon, who went to work for a Fortune 500 company right out of college. He's serious and hard-working, always putting work first. No one salutes the corporate flag faster than he does.

But Sam's company hires the best. No matter how many hours he put in, he only made it to middle management. He's been plateaued at the same rank for about twelve years.

Profit margins have been under terrific pressure and the company's been downsizing for a few years. Sam's boss recently told him he was eligible for an early retirement package. Sam protested, "I don't want to retire. I'm only fifty-two. If I'm not here, where am I going to go? What am I going to do?"

Sam's boss said, "Sam, I can't tell you what to do. But I do know there's a chance your job is going to be eliminated. If you turn the retirement down, you'll have a job even if yours is cut. But I can't tell you what it will be or where it will be."

Sam is taking the package. He will get 60 percent of his salary and full health benefits for the rest of his life. Very indignantly, he told a friend, "Do you know what they just did? They cut my salary by 40 percent!"

What Entitlement Costs Us

The dollar cost of retirement packages to entitled employees is only one reason we cannot afford to tolerate conditions of Entitlement. The real cost to our nation is the loss of productivity, innovation, and creative thinking. Organizations will do better, will have more creative solutions to their issues, when they require performance. Morale is highest and people produce more and are most creative when there is pressure to perform.

Effect on Work Force

We psychologists have long been concerned with the debilitating effects of too much anxiety and we know that productivity suffers when uncertainty is high. But we've failed to realize the equally destructive effects of too little anxiety.

People are not at their keenest when life is too safe. When people receive without having to achieve they are protected from failure. There's no punishment for not achieving. At first glance that may seem like a good thing, but it is not. By protecting people from risk, we destroy their self-esteem. We rob them of the opportunity to become strong, competent people.

Facing risk is the only way we gain confidence, because confidence is the result of mastering challenge. Confidence is an internal state. It cannot be given; it can only be earned. The only way to get genuinely confident is to be familiar with fear and then conquer it. In order to learn we must also occasionally fail. We get courage, the strength to do something new, only when we have learned to see a failure as a battle and not the war. Without courage, no one takes risks; without taking risks, no one develops courage.

Thus, too little anxiety is destructive. It deprives people of the experiences that create confidence. They never learn how to push past risk to success. They never have the opportunity to develop skills of coping, of somehow managing to pull it off even when being unsure.

Instead of strength, courage, and confidence, people trapped by Entitlement are cautious and avoid risk. When security is very high and people shouldn't be afraid, they are. Entitled people cling to Entitlement, fearing they couldn't earn or compete or survive on their own. The long-term result of too much protection is an endless search for protection because you're afraid of losing it.

In the short run, requiring that people earn what they receive is vastly harsher than simply giving it to them. But in the long run, it is the only way that people can gain self-esteem and independence.

Effect on Productivity

If all this seems a bit too psychological, let me put it very concrete, bottom-line terms: When people are not held accountable for performance levels, they don't perform. Instead, they become complacent ("I've got it made") or apathetic ("If it doesn't matter one way or the other, why try? Who cares?").

What happens to involvement and motivation if we have a nation of people saying "Who cares?" What happens to productivity?

Productivity is always low whenever there is Entitlement.

We must shake loose the psychology of Entitlement. We must empower people by giving them responsibilities and we must hold them accountable for their actions. Only in this way can we engender the achievement, growth, and confidence that are necessary for maximum productivity.

Breaking the Cycle

Quite simply, American business and industry can no longer afford to sustain Entitlement. We cannot continue to carry underproductive people. Today, as the rate of change grows continuously faster, we need people who are confident enough to cope with tomorrow's unpredictable problems. People who have been entitled find themselves without the skills they need to cope with changes. They don't have the discipline to persevere, the confidence to withstand uncertainty, or the courage to initiate and innovate. We have reached a critical junction.

Uprooting Entitlement is not easy. It's hard to get people to give up the warm blanket of protection. People who have been accustomed to years of Entitlement will resist increments of risk. They will resist accountability and flee from evaluations. People naturally gravitate to the setting where they feel most comfortable or secure, and they will fight any change from that. That's why Entitlement is so hard to uproot.

To make things even tougher, wherever Entitlement exists it is usually codified in the organization's rules and enshrined in its culture. Thus, it often takes a significant shock to the system, the motivation of crisis, to change things. Since moving away from Entitlement by definition requires risk taking, it will always involve fear. That is the subject of the next chapter.

3

When Organizations Are Too Stressed—The Paralysis of Fear

George Beeler knows about fear. A skilled tool and die maker who has worked in the automobile industry for thirty years, he remembers "when Detroit defined the physical laws of the auto universe." Today, however, the competitive pressure is so bad that "no union could help him now."

George works for a supplier to Ford. Ford is currently trying to develop more Japanese-style supplier relationships: long-term partnerships with fewer suppliers. In endless dread, Beeler constantly rehearses the scene when an irritatingly young inspector from Ford is going to stand in the middle of the shop floor and announce that since his company failed Ford's quality test, it is being dropped. If Ford drops this supplier, George's employer will close down. He says:

> I don't know what will happen. I'm just fighting for my life. I'm not scared of changing. I just want the opportunity to survive. I'm a tiny part of a big machine and I can't tell who's running things. Detroit? Washington? Tokyo? We're all under the ax right now. You drop that ax on these companies, and you're dropping the ax on a whole damn world. That's the world of my father and my son. That's my world.

An employee of a large utility company knows about fear:

> I'd feel more happy in my job if I knew I wasn't going
> to get laid off. . . . I could work better . . . now I have
> stomachaches all the time 'cause I'm always wonder-
> ing. I'm not kidding. I have an ulcer wondering what's
> going to happen. In the past there was a lot of satis-
> faction knowing there was job security and you could
> perform with no risk. Now you could lose your job
> even if you do hustle. My supervisor asked me if I'd
> like to become a supervisor. You got to be kidding.
> That's like cutting off your own throat . . . because
> those are the guys they're laying off. When you're out
> there working, you need your mind on what you're
> doing, and not worrying about "Are you going to lose
> your job tomorrow?"

Layoffs, or the specter of layoffs, are a very real source of
fear. And there is no end in sight. For four years in a row
(1987–90), according to surveys by the American Management
Association, roughly a third of American companies cut their
payrolls. In late 1990, journalist Ron Zemke noted that esti-
mates of how many managers have been cut since the 1981–82
recession vary from 1.5 to 3 million. Cuts are being made in
corporations, governments, quasi-governmental organizations
like the post office, hospitals, universities, and nonprofit asso-
ciations and foundations. And these cuts are not restricted to
the United States. Downsizing is happening in Canada, En-
gland, Holland, and even Japan. Zemke reports that even
among lifetime employers like Sony, Mitsubishi, Honda, and
Toyota, there are "moves afoot" to cut the ranks of professionals
and managers. Japanese basic industries, like steel, have gone
through severe restructurings in order to maintain profits and
markets.

What Fear Is Like

Layoffs, hostile takeovers, and massive corporate restructuring
are tangible. The fear they create is easy to see. People talk

about fear of losing their jobs, or frustration that promotion opportunities have diminished, or resentment as they're asked to contribute more to their health insurance. While those are certainly real issues, they are also the specific expression of a generalized anxiety that can paralyze people and companies.* When people are frozen, waiting for the ax to fall, they don't get much work done.

The crux of excessive anxiety is the feeling that you have no control over what is happening to you. You cannot even influence what's happening. At work, it's as though the playing field is no longer level. You no longer have a manageable deal. You've lost the sense that if you do your part, you can make it okay. You've lost the feeling that you know the rules. Anxiety makes people feel like victims.

Fear in Our Organizations

When anxiety is high, cynicism rises and morale sinks. Inevitably that has a powerful effect on people's dedication to the organization. Companies will not get gung-ho performance from people who are scared, cynical, resentful, apathetic, and mistrustful.

In a study conducted in 1989 and repeated in 1990, the Philadelphia outplacement firm Right Associates reported that human resources executives in 500 companies cited aftershocks from downsizing that profoundly affected everyone involved. They saw low morale in surviving employees, fear of future cuts, and mistrust of management (74 percent in 1989, 80 percent in 1990). Middle managers appear more stressed, seem

---

*In this book I usually use the term *Fear* for this paralyzing anxiety because we all understand what the word means. From a psychological standpoint, anxiety is different from fear. Fears are specific: "I'm afraid to lose my job because a new one might mean moving." Anxiety, in contrast, is generalized: "When I think about losing my job I get sick to my stomach, because without that, there's nothing to hang on to." Fears are concrete; anxiety is pervasive. Anxiety is a whole lot worse than fear. Fears can be transformed into specific issues to be dealt with. Anxiety is the amorphous feeling that something is terribly wrong, and it is this anxiety that we see in many restructuring organizations.

tired all the time, are stretched thin, and seem to be close to burnout. They act as though they have less control over what's going on around them.

In another poll conducted by Right Associates, 74 percent of senior managers at recently downsized companies said that their workers had low morale, feared future cutbacks, and distrusted management. Consultant Gary Neilson of Booz Allen & Hamilton in Chicago said, "The whole quality of decision-making suffers. Employees are always looking over their shoulders. Managers are afraid to take risks."

Fear Smothers Productivity

The significant point for U.S. business is, of course, that downsizing has a direct, bottom-line relationship to productivity. During the height of the layoffs at GE, when people expected productivity to soar, productivity crept along at a disheartening rate of 2.5 percent annually. Some companies have tried to estimate the cost of doom and gloom. In 1987, Bell & Howell was in a three-way takeover skirmish for half the year and rumors of layoffs were everywhere. Everyone felt too depleted and dispirited to work much. Bell & Howell executives have estimated that the drop in productivity for that half year may have cut profits by 11 percent, or $2.1 million.

Writing in *Fortune,* Ronald Henkoff says:

> Administered in repeated doses, [downsizing] can hurt product quality, alienate customers, and actually cut productivity growth. It can foster an organization so preoccupied with bean counting, so anxious about where the ax will fall next, that employees become narrow-minded, self-absorbed, and risk-averse. . . .
> More than half the 1,468 restructured companies surveyed by the Society for Human Resource Management reported that employee productivity either stayed the same or deteriorated after the layoffs.

The Changing Contract

While most employees fully understand the reason for the changes in the old employment contract that promised almost complete job security, still for many these changes feel like a betrayal of trust. Especially for those facing a loss of security or jobs, the changes are experienced emotionally as a breaking of faith. When you can no longer count on the institution that was your emotional center, what can you count on?

The new contract is well illustrated by what happened at AT&T. Before the divestiture in 1984, the giant phone company was a stable organization that offered lifetime employment. The company imposed universal standards that permitted no deviance and created standards of service that required shelves of rule books.

Now AT&T operates in a wholly competitive environment and the competition is global, not just domestic. It's had two major layoffs, early retirement, acquisitions, sales, and mergers. Now it is competing for customers. When you're trying to keep customers, your people have to be flexible. They can't be continuously thumbing through the rule books.

The old AT&T gave people immense psychological security because they were told exactly what to do in every imaginable circumstance. The new AT&T is now telling people to do the reverse. From a risk aversive culture where mistakes were punished, AT&T is trying to become a gutsy place that rewards innovation and decisiveness. No wonder long-term employees are feeling uncomfortable.

"The old company cared," they say. "The new company doesn't. Now, when I can't be sure my job is safe, how do I know I can trust you?"

It is the beginning of the psychology of Fear: The old rules are gone and the new rules don't make sense.

What Panicked People Do

The essence of Fear, remember, is the sense that you have no control over what's happening to you. When people feel powerless, they are preoccupied with issues of power because they never feel safe. Their antennae are constantly sweeping the air, testing for other peoples' intentions. They're forever scanning for subtle cues of coercion, of malevolence, of territorial incursion, of exertions to control them. Psychologically battered, they often become:

Narcissistic:	"I'm watching out for number one."
Paranoid:	"I think everyone's out to get me."
Territorial:	"I'm grabbing my turf and surrounding it with barbed wire."
Rigid:	"I'm hanging on to what I know."
Cynical:	"I'll believe it when I see it."
Political:	"I'm keeping my eyes open."

Denial

Facing enormous, life-shattering changes, the first thing many people do is deny that anything has changed, that anything is wrong. When Fear has replaced Entitlement, people try to re-create their sense of being in control and being secure.

Resistance to change is normal behavior, because change is inherently stressful. In Fear, there's so much stress that people can resist even acknowledging it.

Worry

Whenever people or organizations are in Fear, they will be hypersensitive to the possibility that there's more bad news. Fear generates fear. Thus, when anxiety increases, so do rumors. No one knows what's happening. People make up worst-case scenarios. They're nervous and jerky. They look for commiseration. They complain on the phone and they mythologize the past when everything was great. Sometimes management tries to sustain employee morale by denying that anything is wrong, in turn creating a vacuum that becomes filled with rumors.

A former CBS employee described what things were like at the height of the network's cost cutting:

> There were a couple of months where we sat around and worried all day. Then we started to worry that we were worrying too much, so we went back to work for

ten minutes. Then somebody would call up and say, "Did you see the papers this morning? Are you getting laid off?" So we'd go back to worrying again.

Worried people don't get a lot of work done. Most of their psychological energy is taken up in trying to manage how they feel. When they're worried about themselves, they don't worry about the organization and how it's doing. They're more likely to spend a lot of time in the corridors, at the water cooler, in the cafeteria, or in each other's offices. And they're very likely to put on blank expressions and shut up when the boss is passing by.

Inconsistent Behavior Patterns

When people are in Fear, their behavior is often extreme and frequently inconsistent. Sometimes they'll acknowledge their issues and often they won't. People will alternate working harder to try to get things under control with giving up, accepting fate, or denying anything is wrong. As people get closer to burnout, which is the sense of not having *any* control over what happens to them, they often become more passive and less decisive.

In Fear, people can take on too many risks either out of desperation to change the situation or because they feel that things are so bad they can't get much worse. Or people may rigidly and compulsively follow the rules with a ferocious energy that drains them, because unconsciously they are trying to create order out of chaos.

Coping Techniques

Good Behavior

When reality forces people to acknowledge that security is gone, they try to wrest some sense of control from an amorphous universe. Often they do that by being "good." That's why they bite into the rules, clutch the regulations, and repeat things they already know, things they've already mastered.

When people are scared they keep their eyes on the people in power. The ratio of "yes people" rises exponentially. Until people are able to leave the situation, they will try to keep in good graces, so they placate and please those with power. They will try to avoid conflict and disagreement. They will focus on politics, on pleasing their superiors, and they'll avoid the differences in opinion that are the substance of real work.

Self-Protection

Fear often makes people grab on to territory so they have something to control and defend. Everyone else is a potential predator because they're out to protect themselves also, so no one can be trusted. Hal Burlingame, senior vice-president for Human Resources of AT&T, described the effects of divestiture and especially the trauma of downsizing:

> While major corporate upheavals have tended to draw people in other businesses more closely together, circling the wagons, our upheaval has caused the walls between units to become higher and stronger. Rather than drawing together, our people have narrowed their focus and strengthened their allegiance to their own entity, their own department, or their own work unit.

In Fear, there's no real ambition because there's no energy left. Energy is used for hanging on.

After Pacific Gas and Electric downsized, reorganized, and lost its monopoly because of deregulation, anxiety soared. The result, according to more than half of the employees, was a decline in people working together in order to assure the company's interest. Instead, people set out to protect their turf. "We seem to change direction daily, not through creativity and innovation, but through personal power struggles and inefficiency. One of the most significant obstacles facing PG&E employees today is continuing turf battles which hinder communication and cooperation among departments."

When people are scared and clinging to safety there's no

commitment to the whole. You don't get teamwork. As a result, organizational citizenship drops out. People stop helping others, they don't put in more time than is strictly required, and they won't share information.

Unrelenting competition causes the same territorial behavior. People won't cooperate with others and they won't communicate, because helping others improve their performance can jeopardize one's own competitive success. That's the way it's been at GM because the way up the ladder has historically been to outperform colleagues. When Roger Smith was chairman, he said that territorial pride often outweighed the corporate good. "There's some guy out there in an accounts-payable department, looking over that sea of heads bowed down over their little stamps and saying, 'It's mine, all mine.' "

Seeking Safety

When there's a significant increase in uncertainty, there's always a tendency to go back to styles of coping that used to provide comfort.

Some people will try to flee the situation either by actually leaving or through denial, which takes them mentally away from a reality that's overwhelming. Some people become rigid and refuse to do anything they haven't done many times before. GM's Roger Smith has called these people the "frozen middle management." Some people get so scared they don't do anything at all.

When anxiety is very high, some people try to be invisible. They're afraid to be noticed, so they conform even more than before. They're afraid to be visible because the rules aren't clear anymore and they could be seen as deviates, mavericks, or trouble makers.

Scared, because it's no longer possible to know how to get secure, people try to make sure they're not making mistakes. When anxiety is very high, the natural tendency will be for decisions to be pushed higher and higher up the ladder. When anxiety is very high and people want to avoid risks of any kind, they will delegate decisions upward.

Delegating upward, asking for permission, is a way to avoid

risk. A good example took place in one of the regional Bells.
The Bells, as we all know, are trying to shake up the too-secure
culture they inherited from AT&T. Their people know the
right words to say, but it's hard to shake off the cautions of
Entitlement.

Managers in this particular Bell wanted to encourage the
delegation of decision-making downward, so they eliminated an
entire level of management. There had been five levels and now
there were four. The result was that fewer and fewer decisions
got made. After level four was eradicated, everyone who was at
level three went up to level five to get permission to do things.
There weren't enough people at level five to go around.

When anxiety is very high, decision making will increasingly be a function of committees. The result will be committees
that never confront issues or each other. Many decisions will not
be made and those that are will be compromises.

Solace in the Hierarchy

In Fear, people look for support from authority. They seek
solace in the hierarchy. A hierarchy serves many functions. Besides the obvious ones like defining responsibility, increasing
coordination, and assigning decision making, it helps people
deal with anxiety. Hierarchies comfort because they tell people
where they belong and what they are supposed to do. They
provide approval and acceptance from those with greater authority. When anxiety is very high, people need reassurance the
most. Then people are desperate for the assurance from authority that things will be better.

Fear in Action

Now let us see how these psychological truths play out in the
real world. The three companies discussed here are real, and
their industries and the data given are real; the only omissions
are real names.

Energy Company—The Vicious Cycle of Fear

In the early 1980s, one of our largest energy companies was filled with enormous enthusiasm. It had a mission: Through its energy programs it would save the nation!

The corporation had always hired the very best graduates from the very best universities. And the implicit contract was, "Because you're one of the best, and we're going to ask you for some sacrifices, if you work reasonably hard, you'll have an exciting career with positions of responsibility and you'll be paid well. We welcome you on board and expect you'll be with us for a long time. Most of our people stay with us for the whole of their career."

Then, in May 1986, the price of oil plummeted and the corporation announced plans to slash the work force. A "voluntary" retirement program was instituted, budgets were cut, projects were eliminated, and parts of the company were sold or relocated. Although very few people were actually fired, people's perception of their security changed as the company moved from Entitlement to Fear.

Even though it was generally understood why the cutbacks and reorganization were necessary, many still felt betrayed and angry. Since people tend to trust their own managers with whom they've worked, a lot of blame and mistrust were directed at top management.

Employees entered the vicious cycle of Fear. They strategized for their survival by doing only what they were told, taking no risks, and second-guessing everything. As anxiety rose, so did dependence. Their increased need for support from the leadership they did not trust eroded their self-esteem and taught them they were victims. Learned helplessness increased their dependence and victimization. And the cycle continued.

After the reorganization, the corporation's leadership analyzed the reaction of the organization as a whole to the heightened stress. They called it psychic gridlock.

When people stopped trusting the company, they tried to protect their territory by competing for resources, which had several effects. Conflict over resources led to an increase in office politics. Instead of focusing on the needs of the organization, people concentrated on getting what they could get for themselves.

Competition for resources also resulted in a loss of reserves. Combined with the increased office politics, the emphasis was on the short term. The organization as a whole got cautious. No one took risks. People distorted information in order to protect themselves.

Since reserves were down, there was no cushion. Everything became an emergency, so management increased its controls. Power became increasingly centralized, but since caution dominated, there was no horizontal communication and all vertical communication was top-down. The top of the pyramid was ignorant of what was going on below it.

As resources got tighter, management moved to eliminate what it called nonessentials. Some of those were largely symbolic, like personalized notepads. In the face of all the takeaways, morale plummeted and the executives exerted more and more control. The amount of required paperwork grew enormously. With a sort of gallows humor, people talked about having to measure and record "how long the pencils are." Because the situation was not contained, controls increased. There were more surveillance procedures, more rules, and more time spent enforcing rules.

That's when gridlock moved into the full-blown overcontrol syndrome. There was a big increase in pressure to "do what you're told; this is the way we do things." As a result, conformity increased, risk taking declined, communication decreased, rumors increased, and trust, efficiency, and adaptation decreased. The defense—the attempt to cope with anxiety—had become a part of the problem.

Communications Company—The Impact of Unremitting Anxiety

This high-tech communications company was a pioneer in its field. There was a vast and growing market for its products and technology. Before long the company was bought by a much larger, more traditional communications company. The marriage between the original free spirits and the more straitlaced managers of the buyer created enormous anxiety. Then, international competition exploded, diminishing the company's market share. Worse, the core business is now mature and is no longer fast-growing and entrepreneurial. In the start-up days of the company, anxiety could trigger very positive energies. Now anxiety can generate only more anxiety.

Within the company, no critical, final decisions are being made. In fact, none have been made for a long time. Many of the company's original employees have left for other organizations where the future seems surer and there's some sense of control. In the face of anxiety and depression, the surviving employees are laying a lot of blame on the new owner. Whether the company were bought or not, its spirit would no longer be exuberant because it doesn't own the market anymore. But it's not emotionally satisfying to say "Economic conditions have changed!" It's vastly more sustaining to have a living target to blame for trouble.

In this company, sustained depression and prolonged anxiety have resulted in the loss of any sense of membership in a team or being part of an organization. The high levels of anxiety have increased employee preoccupation with what's going to happen to them. Self-absorbed, each individual is separate from everyone else. People feel alone and very vulnerable. While employees are asking the new owner for support and compassion, the buyer is saying "Enough! Move forward. Go!"

Utility Company—Confusion of a New Environment

Before deregulation of the industry, this company had a monopoly on supplying energy to its territory. The monopoly is now gone and the company must find its way through the strange environment of a competitive marketplace.

Employees have remained loyal to this company in the wake of major changes and they want to help make the company successful against the competition, but they are in conflict. They hear the words *market-driven* and they aren't sure how they will be affected. They're feeling anxious because they haven't figured out how to combine the spirit of public service with cost efficiency. They realize the market has become competitive and they need to take moderate risks, but they don't know how. More than anything, they're afraid they're going to lose the soul of their organization. In the midst of the transitions that generate anxiety, they're not sure of the direction management is taking and they're not confident that management knows where it's going.

In the wake of change, the level of trust has declined. The majority of people in the bargaining unit don't feel they're in a trusting work environment, nor does half of middle management, nor do one-third of the executives. The feeling that senior management doesn't trust middle management permeates the organization.

A lack of trust in specifics soon becomes a lack of trust in everything—it becomes generalized. For example, many employees don't trust the credibility of internal corporate publications on sensitive or controversial issues. They think top-down communication can't be trusted. Many are convinced the grapevine is the best source of information on what's happening. And they're cynical about upward communication, because they're convinced no one is listening. Cynicism also becomes generalized: "Management wants us to think they really care about our opinions. But that's only what they want us to think. They're not going to do anything with what we say."

Researchers at the utility company found there were dramatic changes in how employees perceived the company. People were asked to think about the old and the new companies as though they were people and then to describe them in terms of personality qualities. People felt the market-driven strategy changed the organization fundamentally. The words used to describe the old organization were warm and emotional: *family-oriented, caring, loyal, honest, competent,* and *confident.* While they said it was too bureaucratic, they also said it had been a fun, social, family-oriented organization that valued older, experienced people. Now, the rising stars were younger, educated, white-collar yuppies straight out of school. That's why, they said, there's been a decline in competence.

Employees described the new organization as schizophrenic. It has the contradictory qualities of being both authoritarian and entrepreneurial, cautious and innovative. It has kept all the bad qualities of the "old" organization and has lost everything that was positive. It's still bureaucratic, but without any warmth.

They also described the new organization as insecure and chaotic. It's a place of stress, fear, selfishness, and shortsightedness. Most important, employees feel the company has lost its integrity and competence.

Almost half of the employees in this company feel their work is not appreciated and less than a third say they get positive feedback when they do good work. Only 18 percent think good work is rewarded. The great majority, 74 percent, are skeptical that doing a good job will make their future any more secure. Among employees at all levels morale is at an all-time low.

Lessons to Learn

What the Boss Has to Do

In conditions of Fear, there is no trust. In organizations undergoing the turbulence of major change, when employees are least able to trust, that's just when they are being asked to trust their leaders to get them through the period of anxiety.

In such a situation, whoever has more power needs to understand the dysfunctional consequences of feeling that things are out of control. Thus, those in charge shouldn't add to the anxiety.

Some managers and executives try to gain control by becoming tough. Sometimes being tough is the leadership the situation requires. Toughness can be constructive. However, when an organization or an individual is already very anxious, unrelenting and capricious demands will increase the anxiety level.

Peter Nulty found that being tough can be constructive, but it's a high-risk style because "the boss constantly plays chicken with the limits of his subordinate's endurance."

Since there's tremendous resistance to giving up Entitlement, and there will be a continual drift back to the security of Entitlement whenever pressure is lessened, change will require consistent and constructive toughness when it comes to requiring performance and resisting dependence. But when anxiety is already high and the need is to move from Fear, the most effective style will use reasonable, predictable, and articulated psychological support, conveying, especially, the ways in which security can be earned.

The Positive Side of Anxiety

The 1980s were a time of crisis. Many of our institutions needed to change and many more still do. In effect, they have to pay for the accumulated inefficiencies that Entitlement permitted. In a market economy, old structures and techniques are destroyed and replaced when they no longer function well. Though the process is often painful, the result is a dynamic renewal.

This period of turbulence, then, is an awful ending of some certainties and assumptions. There is the end of job security for people at all levels, the end of certainty about the future, and the early end of promotion for many. Those ends must be accepted as ends and must be converted to beginnings. Those ends are the opportunities for organizations to get lean and to push power down.

As long as it is not so high as to be disabling, Fear is the great motivator. While it is true that the restructuring and the downsizing are causing serious pain, they are also resulting in organizations that are in much better shape to operate in the continuous turbulence of a world economy in the 1990s.

The psychology of Fear can lead to the psychology of Earning, which is the upside of Fear. Once we have a clear vision of what we are doing, we can guide our organizations toward Earning by leading them deliberately but compassionately out of Entitlement through the necessary step of Fear.

Finding just the right level of Fear and managing it is vastly different from watching helplessly as companies flounder under the effects of Fear that come from external economic difficulties. Deliberately, strategically moving organizations from Entitlement to Earning, by way of optimal levels of Fear, is described in later chapters. Probably the greatest of the dangers is the loss of all sense of Fear, because then we will inevitably slide back to the disabling comfort of Entitlement.

4

When Organizations Are Revitalized — The Energy of Earning

In a nondescript building in a commercial section of San Diego, there is a vision of the future, a merger of the baby-boomer ideals of fun and sharing with a tough-minded drive to succeed financially. Industrial Computer Source was formed by a group of people disillusioned with their former employer, a major computer company with a classic Silicon Valley culture.

The company they left is famous. Everyone wears jeans and leaves at 4 P.M. on Fridays for beer. There was supposed to be profit sharing, with employees owning a large portion of the company's stock. The company's president was recently quoted as saying "Working here is like being self-employed."

Although this situation sounds ideal, the vice-president for finance at the new company says, "We worked like dogs in crummy conditions. Supposedly we were all sacrificing for the good of all, but all we were really doing was making the president richer. We made the profits and he got to keep them."

The motto of the old company is "Make do and do without." That would have been fine if there had been a payoff in sight, but there was none.

In six years, the new company has gone from zero to $15 million in sales and has no debt. In 1988, thirty-one people earned a total of $1.3 million. Pretax profit in 1990 was $2.4

million. At the end of every shipping day the profits for the day are posted.

One of the founders says:

> The profit is handed down right away and it's not in stock options. Everyone knows how much money we've made. At the end of the quarter, everyone gets a piece of it. Immediately. We never had a quarter with a loss. Hourly people get a month's pay and the rest of us get 10 percent.
>
> Not only that, we pay 110 percent of the top price for salaries for all positions. So even if the owner— and there is one guy who owns most of it—even if he didn't give you a bonus, you'd still have made more money than you could have anywhere else. We expect everyone to work like hell. That's part of the deal and everybody knows it.
>
> We got terrific people here and they're here because they want to be part of the next phase because we're growing so fast. If we grow, we're geniuses. If we don't, we'll be in trouble with the special people we hired. But we tell the truth and everyone knows what's happening, so I think we'll be okay.
>
> There's a difference between financial and psychological equity. In the other company, they talked both and delivered on neither. We're trying to do both, but especially financial. The psychological stuff just happens. At the end of the day I'm physically tired because I worked for ten hours. But I'm not emotionally tired. Our success is tangible so we feel competent and optimistic.
>
> We've got a pleasant environment and nice people. Ultimately the president says "go/no go" or "spend/don't spend," but for the most part we all do whatever we have to. Everybody does whatever is necessary.
>
> When we moved into this building, everybody got in and cleaned and painted. The president too. We had vice-presidents making shelves along with assem-

blers. We didn't want the niggardly mentality of the other company here so we got nice space.

I found the new space notable for its nondescriptness. In front, there are some ordinary parking spaces; none are reserved. Inside, there's little physical evidence of status. It's a reflection of the relative unimportance of hierarchy.

Of course, there is a hierarchy. There's a president who put up most of the money; he owns more of the company than anyone else. Some officers who were founders have a significant share. There are many others who have no shares. In terms of how everyone works, hierarchical power is pretty unnecessary. In practice, most of the time, no one works for someone else. People don't ask what their job is; they find out what needs to be done. In general terms, they are told what they're supposed to accomplish. Then they go and do it. More than anything, there's camaraderie in the pursuit of more success.

Competition is a terrific motivator in the new company. It has gained a lot of energy from its desire to prove something to the old company. Because employees felt betrayed, this competition is partly fueled by vengeance. The synergy of successful growth and successful vengeance is powerful.

As an organization the company is winning because it's getting bigger faster than the old company. Within a few years at this rate of growth, it will overtake the old company. When it's bigger than the old company, it's going to take on the industry leader. War is fun when you're winning.

Everyone who works at Industrial Computer Source feels like a winner. The products stand ready to be shipped, right near the offices. The offices are off a corridor near the assembly room. The lunch room is right in the middle. It's bright and clean inside, lit by the southern California sun. Posted on the wall for everyone to see are yesterday's numbers.

The Essence of Earning

What we are seeing in Industrial Computer Source is an organization experiencing the natural high of success, of Earning.

The climate of Earning is purposeful, disciplined energy. In start-up companies like Industrial Computer Source, the environment itself provides the stimulus. In more mature organizations, enlightened leaders will have to engineer the conditions that create Earning.

An Earning environment requires realistic opportunities to achieve and realistic requirements to do so. It requires parameters of achievement so there's pressure to perform and some certainty when you have performed. It requires accurate matching of requirements to ability so that you're right more often than you're wrong.

People with a psychology of Earning know they're winners, but they also know they're always being judged. Although past achievements get you into today's game, only today's achievements will get you into tomorrow's game. Earning is the end result of a continuous tension in which people are under pressure to perform, but they have the means to reduce the pressure through achievement.

And they are not afraid. To people with a mind-set of Earning, that medium level of pressure makes things exciting. They have learned that change is an opportunity to experience challenge, and that mastering challenge is the only way to *earn* the experience of being right, of being first, of being a winner.

Thus, a psychology of earning is a psychology of winning. People discover that when they accept risk, they benefit. They develop techniques to cope with the stress, and uncertainty is not as frightening to them. They will face increased challenge by attempting to achieve more.

The attitude of Earning recognizes this basic fact of human psychology: People prefer accountability; they want to be rewarded when they work hard and they want those who don't to be punished. They want their work to be judged because it is the only way to feel that their work is significant. People with a psychology of Earning will tend not to respect people who don't earn their success. For them, trying is not enough; accomplishment will be a requirement for respect.

Therefore, this attitude requires that people begin with some level of self-confidence and are willing to work to acquire more. Being willing to be judged takes courage and it takes confidence.

The only people able to move beyond the psychologies of Entitlement or Fear are those who have achieved enough to feel confident. Confidence is empowering. Empowered, people feel able to take on more risks. They become better able to earn and accept responsibility and autonomy. They feel that they're heard, they're involved, they're effective, they make decisions, and they make a difference. Taking on risk, working, and then succeeding creates more of a sense of empowerment. It's a wonderful, energizing cycle of positive accomplishments.

Practical Benefits

Organizations that have or create an Earning environment reap increased productivity, increased innovation, and increased teamwork. It's not hard to see that an energized work force contributes directly to the bottom line.

Productivity

Americans traditionally believed that all people should earn their own way. That was a moral judgment, but we didn't realize that it was also an enabling point of view. Being held to task is the only way people can develop confidence and independence. It's also the only condition under which larger systems can be productive.

The equivalent of productivity in an organization is problem solving by an individual. In both cases, the result is confidence and thus courage. That's why we say that the psychology of Earning is the real secret of productivity. Only where there's a psychology of Earning do people achieve, solve problems, move forward, change, and adapt. Problems are not solved and anxiety is not reduced by hugging trees or bureaucratic security blankets. With an attitude of Earning you articulate the problem, address it directly, and solve it incrementally.

Innovation

In these days of make-or-break competition, it is particularly worth noting the connection between Earning and innovation. Earning and empowerment are preconditions for creativity, especially when big breakthroughs are involved. Creativity involves what psychologists call "breaking set," seeing things differently from how they've been seen before. Breaking set involves taking a risk because being different is usually perceived initially as being wrong.

Confidence is the critical ingredient in being able to leave the security of what's known and familiar and move into the new and unfamiliar. Only people who have earned confidence will be able to stop clinging to precedent and relying on rules. Confidence earned through the experience of achieving is a prerequisite for being able to disagree, especially with those people who have greater power. Only when people feel respected for what they've achieved can they give up the safety of being "yes people."

In Earning organizations there may be rules, but it's understood that rules may be broken because circumstances are always changing. People are encouraged to ask "Do we do what we did before, or do we try something new? Do we follow precedent or do we have to bend or ignore the rule?" This kind of questioning frees people from confinement, so they are psychologically able to deviate from what occurred before and they are therefore better able to be creative or innovative.

Teamwork

In this kind of environment, teamwork flourishes. The effective team is made up of individuals who are confident in their talent. While individuals are capable of being innovators, their esteem makes it possible for them to work collaboratively, disciplined under someone's leadership for the good of the whole. Teams are most successful when the members are entrepreneurs but are willing to harness their ability to the unit's purposes and capabilities.

Respect for the other person's contribution is the real basis of teamwork. It isn't the result of a particular method of operating but rather the result of a fundamental attitude: "Other people know something I'll benefit from hearing." Teamwork is the expression of a willingness to collaborate because you respect the others. All those involved in making decisions have earned that right and are comfortable with the responsibility and the power. They're also comfortable because they're very confident in their ability.

You can't have a team psychology when people are preoccupied with protecting themselves. Management exhortations or training for team skills are nonproductive in Entitlement or Fear because in both cases people are too insecure to be able to contribute to the well-being of others. They can't risk the possibility that others might end up looking better.

Where there is a psychology of Earning, people feel they're part of a community. Because they don't feel the need to gain more power to protect themselves, people are able to hear others. When you can hear, you're better able to appreciate the needs of and work to the betterment of the team or the organization as a whole. Team members are competitive in the sense that no one wants to look bad in front of the people they respect. Everyone's opinion is on the table where it will be judged by everyone else. There's electricity in the air because opinions are always being evaluated and challenged. Because people are not defensive, no one needs to win at the expense of the others.

Thus, people in empowered teams are colleagues at the same time they are competitors. It's what I call creative tension—that mixture of cooperation and competition that leads to attempts at improvement, to the end of complacency, to the drive to innovation and ever-better decisions.

This blend of competition and cooperation is probably optimal in raising effort and productivity to their highest levels. As people find their team creates more excitement and far better performance than they had as individuals, it becomes easier to contribute selflessly to the team. Team commitment is also greater when individuals have the opportunity to feel that they are successful in the team and that the team is a successful competitor.

Motivation for Excellence

When we think about what we need to do to create and sustain high levels of morale in organizations, we never think of hard work and pressure to produce. And yet, where would you expect morale to be higher? In a rich organization where carpets are deep and walls are paneled and there's all the time in the world to investigate and discuss and write reports, or in a brand-new entrepreneurial organization where people are putting in sixteen-hour days and the whole thing will sink or swim depending on the quality and speed with which they can produce a new idea and get the product out?

The best morale builder, the greatest motivator, is success, that is, earning the status of being a winner.

To create the climate where this attitude can thrive, we must understand what drives people to Earning behaviors. What motivates good work? What provides a sense of enrichment and fulfillment?

In the past twelve years I have given hundreds of seminars and workshops on career and life plateauing, and I always ask people "What do you require from your work to feel satisfied?" People are encouraged to call out their responses, and time after time they tend to name the same things. No matter what type of organization or industry, whether I'm talking to managers or professionals or line workers, there's tremendous consistency in what people say. Three conditions are needed in order for employees to feel enriched:

Challenge:	To risk and learn and fulfill their potential
Empowerment:	To be autonomous so they can be creative, make decisions, and act
Significance:	To do things that matter and create value

These are also the three ingredients of Earning. In companies where a psychology of Earning exists, people have what they need to do good work. Thus, the task of leaders and managers is to nurture and maintain those three ingredients. (Specific techniques are presented in Chapter 8; for now, I simply want to point out the link between job satisfaction and the psychology of Earning.)

Challenge

People describe what challenge means to them in these words:

"I want to keep on learning."
"I want to use my talents."
"I want different responsibilities."
"I want to feel like I'm fulfilling my potential."
"I want every day to be different."
"I want to master new things."
"I want to keep on growing."
"I want some risk."
"I want it to be fun!"

To get commitment and high performance, organizations must make sure employees have the chance to tackle challenging experiences in which they stretch, learn, risk—and succeed.

Empowerment

When people describe what empowerment means to them, they say:

"I want to make decisions."
"I need to be autonomous."
"I want to be able to act."
"I like to be on the leading edge."
"I need to be creative."
"I want to innovate."
"I need to lead."
"I want people to respect me."
"I want authority."
"I need flexibility."
"I don't want to have to ask permission."
"I don't want to have to go by the book."
"I want to be responsible."
"I want to be accountable."

When people are given opportunities to organize and make decisions appropriate to their knowledge and experience, they usually move up to the opportunity. They think for themselves, they sharpen their skills, they focus their efforts, and they display grit and self-control. Given the chance, freed from the restrictions of the hierarchy, sustained by the group, they move further into the psychology of Earning.

The payoff for organizations is tremendous. Jack Welch, the CEO of General Electric, says "If we let our people flourish and grow, if we use the best ideas they come up with, then we have the chance to win [in global competition]. The idea of liberation and empowerment for our work force is not enlightenment—it's a competitive necessity."

Significance

Most people want their work to be significant. They're asking that their work contribute to something they feel is important:

"I want to do things that matter."
"I want to feel I've achieved, I've accomplished, I've made a difference."
"I want excellence."
"I need to create value."
"What I do is important work."
"I don't just shuffle paper."
"I'm in the mainstream."
"I make an impact."
"There's a purpose to what I do."
"I'm contributing to something important."
"My work makes me feel like I'm a good person."

In an interview in *Harvard Business Review,* Paul Cook, CEO of Raychem Corporation, was asked how he keeps his people motivated over the long haul:

Most people, whether they're engineers, business managers, or machine operators, want to be creative.

They want to identify with the success of their profes-
sion and their organization. They want to contribute
to giving society more comfort, better health, more
excitement. And their greatest reward is receiving
acknowledgment that they did contribute to making
something meaningful happen. So the most important thing we do is build an organization—a culture,
if you'll pardon the word—that encourages teamwork, that encourages fun and excitement, that encourages everyone to do things differently and better—and that acknowledges and rewards people who
excel.

Creating an Organization of Winners

Psychological research tells us that motivation is highest when
the probability of success is 50 percent: We don't get involved if
the task is too easy or too hard. At its core, then, creating the
conditions of Earning means moving people into a middle
range of risk—increasing pressure if people are stuck in Entitlement, or decreasing pressure if they are paralyzed by Fear—
while supporting their efforts.

Reaching that middle point may take a significant push.
Since nothing is more confidence-building than facing risk directly and managing it, people who avoid risk have to be required to move into it. If organizations don't require the
stretch, people can be cheated of the sense of accomplishment
that comes from pushing beyond what's comfortable.

The goal is not to create Fear, which would be unproductive. Rather it is that medium level of risk that stimulates
achievement. That's why clever organizations continuously increase the requirements of performance. If you set those goals
within the reach of a stretch, the negative pressure has a positive outcome because the level of accomplishment becomes a
triumph. IBM calls it "raising the bar" and the targets are set
so that 90 percent of the people can attain them.

To illustrate the effective use of anxiety leading to success,
my favorite example is the boot camp training of the Marine

Corps. (I'm not prescribing military service. I'm simply observing the Marine Corps' very successful use of manageable anxiety to achieve a goal.)

San Diego is home for one of the largest boot camps of the Corps. Whenever I fly home, there are always some Marine recruits on the plane. Adolescents, they come in many assorted and ill-fitted sizes: skinny and weak, fat and sloppy, pimply and awkward. I look at these kids and I think, "*You* are going to defend me?" Twelve weeks later they are not recognizable. They stand tall. They walk with controlled power. They project confidence. The change is awesome.

How do the Marines do it? The drill instructor (DI) pushes as hard as possible, using as much top-down power, as much authority, as possible. That amount of authority takes the recruits into very high levels of anxiety. In our model, they go into Fear. But the Marine Corps has also created the mechanism by which the Boots can earn their way out of anxiety.

The DI teaches the recruits not to fail the platoon. Under the conditions of Fear, the recruits are offered a hand: If they relate to each other, if they bond together, if each individual's loyalty is to the unit, then each individual has access to support from the whole group when needed.

The Marines use fear and competition to create high anxiety. They use high anxiety to create bonding. The bonding results both in peer support and peer pressure to perform. The combined peer support and pressure result in high performance. High performance creates the sense of being empowered, of being confident. Sustained empowerment and performance result in a psychology of Earning. What a training program!

5

Understanding How People Work—The Earning Curve

Everything discussed so far can be summarized in one simple drawing. If we make a graph with productivity on one plane and pressure (anxiety, risk, stress, fear—here they all mean the same) on the other, and draw in the familiar bell-shaped curve (see Fig. 5-1), we can see how productivity and anxiety relate:

Productivity is very low when the level of stress is either very low or very high.

The graph is what social scientists call a model—a way of displaying relationships in visual format. I developed the model from my observations about how people behave and also from two other sources.

The first is the Yerkes-Dodson law, sometimes cited as the only example of a really scientific psychological law, stating that "Anxiety improves performance until a certain optimum level of arousal has been reached. Beyond that point, performance deteriorates as higher levels of anxiety are attained."

The second source is the research done by David Mc-Clelland of Harvard University and John Atkinson of the University of Michigan. They found that motivation to achieve and level of effort keep rising until the expectancy of success (or the level of uncertainty) reaches 50 percent. Then, even though the expectancy continues to increase, motivation falls. When the

Figure 5-1. Levels of productivity as a response to anxiety.

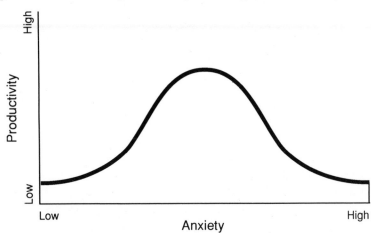

goal is seen as too easy (too certain) or too difficult (too uncertain), there is no motivation or effort.

Though they're not discussing exactly the same variables, these two models converge: The relationships they're describing can be drawn as bell-shaped curves.

If we then superimpose the three psychological conditions on our basic bell curve graph, we get Figure 5-2. On the left

Figure 5-2. Entitlement, Earning, and Fear.

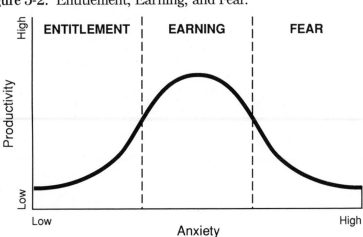

Figure 5-3. The Earning curve as a verbal profile.

WHAT ENTITLEMENT LOOKS LIKE

High Levels	*Low Levels*
Risk avoidance	Flexibility
Avoiding assessment	Accountability
Dependence, passivity	Morale and motivation
Apathy, complacency	Firing
Conformity, rule following	Innovation
Bureaucracy	Empowerment
High number of rules and procedures	Evaluation
High number of rule checkers	Confidence in subordinates

Bottom line: Avoiding risk and creating safety are institutionalized in rules and procedures. Appearance is more important than achievement.

WHAT EARNING LOOKS LIKE

Low Levels	*High Levels*
Self-protection	Trust
Apathy	Accountability
Dependence	Innovation
Following precedent	Leadership
Passivity	Risk taking
	Involvement
	Teamwork
	Decision making
	Motivation
	Excitement

Bottom line: The motive to achieve is high because achieving is possible and security depends on producing.

WHAT FEAR LOOKS LIKE

Low Levels	*High Levels*
Security	Anxiety, uncertainty
Control	Despair

(continued)

Figure 5-3 *(continued).*

Low Levels	High Levels
Morale	Stress
Teamwork	Self-protection
Trust	Dependence
Respect for leaders	Cynicism
Citizenship behavior	Turf protecting
	Denial
	Vulnerability

Bottom line: There is no sense of having any control. People panic and it's every person for himself.

---

side of the curve, anxiety is very low and productivity is very low. This is the Entitlement section of the graph. In the center section, anxiety is moderate and productivity is highest. This section represents the psychology of Earning. On the right side of the graph, anxiety is very high and productivity is very low. This section describes the psychology of Fear.

We will come back to this three-segment curve and will add another layer of information, but first I want to present another way to understand the relationship between anxiety and productivity. In Figure 5-3, the behaviors that you might see under the three different conditions are presented as a kind of verbal profile.

Nine Points on the Earning Curve

Now we can take the model one step further and identify more closely where a person or an organization is on the spectrum. Using a curve makes us realize there are degrees of the psychological states. This is true whether we're talking about an individual in an organization or an organization as a whole. I have assigned numbers to areas along the curve (see Fig. 5-4).

Figure 5-4. The Earning curve.

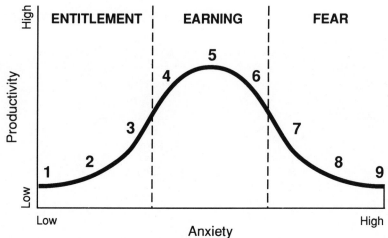

Throughout the rest of the book you'll find these numbers, for example:

"I think I'm a 4."
"That company is a 7."
"My first supervisor was a 2."

The numbers are a relative measure of where an item is on the scale.

As complex as a model may appear, reality is always much more complicated because people or institutions are rarely pure examples of a single state. Instead, you'll usually find they have a strong central tendency that is akin to one place on our curve, and also other aspects of attitudes or behaviors that are closer to other places. Nonetheless, it is possible to generalize about each of the nine points and to describe what they are like.

The descriptions are divided into two general categories: what organizations are like at the nine points and what individuals are like at those same points. As you will see when we begin developing a strategy for change, it is important to be clear whether the problem involves an organization or a group of individuals.

What Organizations Are Like

Point 1. Very hard to fire people. Enforcing discipline takes lots of written justification. Promotion mostly based on seniority. Many hierarchical levels. A hierarchical culture in which formal status is extremely important. No risk taking. Many rules. More emphasis on process or procedure than outcome. Lots of paper. Lots of people checking on others. Many studies and pilot efforts. No new decisions. All the time in the world. No energy. Apathy. Precedent is holy. Respect really means Entitlement.

Point 2. Evaluations too positive. Excess graciousness. No disagreements or confrontations. Little distinction in pay between high and low performers. Looking busy is highly valued so there's lots of face time. Empowerment and risk taking are rare. Committees advise but don't decide. Decisions handed up. Emphasis on what people are owed rather than on what they owe. A culture of assumption and precedent. Do it "our way."

Point 3. Informal tenure for everyone. People compete for success but without obvious drive; style is important. Exchanges usually mannered and gracious. Some empowerment but with a leash. Status differences important though lots of work organized in small groups. Little risk-taking. Progress predictable and incremental. Breakthroughs rare so small innovations treated as big deals. Decisions require management sign-off. Criticism of the organization but not enough of a sense of imperative so that significant changes are made. Basically, it's comfortable.

Point 4. Innovators respected but formal position in the hierarchy remains important as a determinant of influence. Impersonal, creative confrontation or probing discussions. Much work organized in teams. Peer pressure important. Decisions typically made by consensus. Time given to analyze and plan. Change typically thoughtful, logical, and incremental. Mood calm but involved.

Point 5. Few levels in the hierarchy. Dynamics of most relationships like those of peers. Many autonomous teams. Few rules; considerable flexibility. Creativity rewarded. Evaluations cover the full range. Significant rewards and punishments according to performance. Organization is performance (or customer) driven. Outcome much more important than process but procedure has a place. A meritocracy; there are many kinds of power. There's trust. Channels of communication are open. Energy of forward momentum toward a successful future; a sense of excitement.

Point 6. There are two different ways organizations function at point 6. In one case, it is the result of uncertainty and risk: There's a lot of challenge in the environment so some elements of security can't be taken for granted, or there's enormous pressure from superiors and peers to perform. In this case, people are very visible in terms of performance and pressure to perform is unremitting. Errors are punished but not as much as not doing one's best. Work comes first. It's assumed to be the most important thing in everyone's life.

The second way is to be an organization that enjoys and prefers to be in a riskier or more entrepreneurial mode. The greatest prestige goes to innovators and creators. Knowledge is power and it's more important than formal status. Evaluations are tough and there are significant rewards and punishments. Decisions are made both by consensus and unilaterally. The pace of change is fast. With few rules, there's little regard for precedent. Deviance is applauded. It's a procedurally or structurally loose organization and it works. The mood is that of high excitement.

Point 7. Discomfort because no one knows the right way to do things. Decisions are pushed up. Efforts made to generate new, more appropriate rules or procedures. Discussion of the future and efforts to create the new vision. Doubt about the future, some skepticism that it can be made to work, some putting down of the leadership, but also some hope. Some of the better people may be leaving. The pendulum of values and goals moves in arcs that are too wide because the preference is for action and there's impatience when solutions are not achieved quickly. High energy level. Tendency to overreact and therefore act precipitously.

Point 8. No sense of security or predictability. Leaders are not leading. Rules and precedents from the past are rarely appropriate now, but there aren't any clear new ones. A lot of floundering. The result is attempts to grab new rules (or a vision or a culture) from somewhere rather than let them evolve. Discussion of future goals but the goals or vision are discounted. Poor morale. Communication is top-down. Decisions rarely made and less frequently implemented. Mood is cynical.

Point 9. Rules from the past in a present that is chaos. No rules that work. No vision, strategy, or leadership. As a result, there's clinging to precedent, old rules, and conforming in the bureaucracy. Decisions not made. No focus. There's either the high energy of panic or the flatness of fatalism. Terrible morale.

Figure 5-5 is an overview of the nine points on the curve as it applies to organizations.

In the same way that we characterized organizations, we can describe the nine facets of the curve as they might be reflected in an individual.

What Individuals Are Like

Point 1. *I have it coming because you owe me.* Panics with risk. Emotion high if there is the perception of any risk, including that of accountability. With risk, this person needs a life-saver. Tendency to deny the loss of entitlement or the requirement for performance. Follows and memorizes the rules. Avoids risk. Apathetic, passive, and dependent though that can be hard to discern under the overt "You owe me" attitude. Intervention is tricky because, with the perception of risk, this person is prone to go from 1 to 9.

Point 2. *I did the best I could so I don't understand why you're crabbing at me.* Resistant to increased risk or accountability. Projects causes from the self and rationalizes failure: "Circumstances were out of my control." May say "This is good enough." Blames others—managers or co-workers—for nonperformance. Very judgmental and frequently verbal. Presumptuous. Greedy. Avoids assessment. Tries to look good. Is prone to justify performance, saying "Look at the time and effort I put in!" Very difficult and time-consuming to deal with because the anxiety is high but so is the denial of any responsibility. Hard to budge from Entitlement.

Figure 5-5. Summary of points on the Earning curve for organizations.

Point	Characteristic
1. A PRECEDENT-DRIVEN BUREAUCRACY that has all the time in the world.
2. A PSEUDOMERITOCRACY of inconsequential evaluations.
3. A sense of COMFORT within GRACIOUS COMPETITION.
4. Incremental progress through TEAMS and CONSENSUAL DECISION-MAKING.
5. EXCELLENCE achieved through CONTINUOUS ADAPTATION to the REALITIES of OUTCOME.
6. INNOVATION, CREATIVITY, and RISK TAKING get the highest marks.
7. OVERREACTING, goals and values CHANGE in BIG ARCS.
8. In crisis, LEADERS and the FUTURE are viewed CYNICALLY.
9. WITHOUT GOALS or LEADERSHIP the present and future feel OUT OF CONTROL.

Point 3. *I can see that things could be better, but you know, I'm really comfortable just the way they are.* Most of these people have had at least some success on the job. They'll accept what they perceive as a reasonable challenge, change, or incremental responsibility. It's not too hard to get their understanding. But, nonetheless, their strategy is to not make waves, keep things agreeable, placate the boss, and resist real change, including accountability. While they give lip service to the need for improvement, basically they're complacent. They'd like to keep things as they are.

Point 4. *Change is good, but haste gets you in trouble. Take the time to think things through.* These people work well, know they're competent, aren't afraid of change, but prefer to study the situation from many different angles before proceeding. Comfortable disagreeing with others in discussion, but prefer consensus rather than dictating to others. Prefer working with others and organize in teams.

Point 5. *I'm doing this as well as I can. There's only one standard of performance, and that's doing one's best. I can't help it—I'm natu-*

rally competitive. I go for excellence! These people have attitudes, behaviors, and confidence that are optimal. As a result, they're flexible and adaptive. Aware of precedent but keep on learning. Disciplined in the pursuit of achievement. Responsible; autonomous and collaborative in turn, depending on circumstances. Initiating and decisive but trusting. Listen to others. Tell the truth. Optimistic, they're goal- and future-oriented.

Point 6. *I don't like doing things in dribs and drabs. When there's a need to do it, then do it! It's really fun to go out and hook horns with the big guys. If there's a chance, I'd rather go for the big one!* These people seek risk and may even create it. Dislike the assumption that following the rules is best. Comfortable deviating and may be creative. Often prefer to work alone, at least in analyzing or planning, and join with others only for implementation.

Point 7. *There's so much going on, there's so much coming down, you don't know what's going to happen. You can't let your guard down and you can never let up.* Too competitive, uneasy and stressed, this person isn't a good team player. Though too tense for optimal performance, not far from the success pattern. Need reassurance. In this case, the reassurance most needed is that they can meet challenge, they can succeed, and when they do, they'll regain a sense of having control over what's happening. Relatively easy to reassure.

Point 8. *Things are really scary out there. You can't trust anyone. What kind of lies am I being fed? You better be prepared. You better watch out!* This person grabs territory (i.e., budget and head count) and gets political (i.e., seeks power and supporters). Judgmental and emotional; blames the leadership (or parents). "Everything was better before." Narcissistic, cynical, and mistrustful. Hard to deal with. Time-consuming. Underlying his or her fears, there's often rage.

Point 9. *It's so awful I can't think about this. It's so terrible, there's no way out. There's nothing I can do. Help me, help me! Make me safe.* There's so much fear that it's become a generalized anxiety; a pervasive sense of doom. People are often paralyzed, incapable of doing anything purposeful. Cling to what they've already mastered; survive by scooting along the top of reality, never looking at it, never dealing with it. Self-preoccupied, there's a constant search for support and reassurance. Whatever the overt behavior, there's panic. Intervention is crucial. Offered a hand, they may cling like a limpet.

Figure 5-6 summarizes these levels.

Try your hand at the model; it's fun, and it will help solidify the concept. For example, where would you put:

> United States? (in my workshops, usually 2 or 3)
> Japan? (usually 4 or 5)
> Your company?
> Your part of the business?
> Your boss?
> Your direct reports?
> The person at the next desk?
> Yourself?

Mismatch Between Individuals and Companies

We have to distinguish between where an organization might be on the Earning curve and where individuals are. The level of

Figure 5-6. Attitudes on the Earning curve.

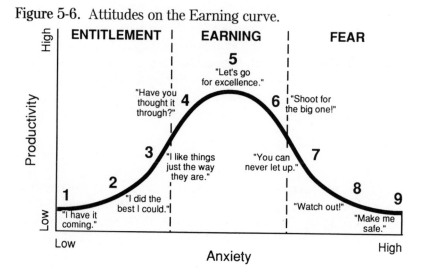

anxiety present in the culture of any organization will affect the uncertainty of the individuals within it, but not all individuals will have the same level of anxiety. While there may be conditions that create an overall psychology of Entitlement, individuals within those circumstances may have a psychology of Earning or even of Fear.

There are large differences in how people experience risk. Some people find small amounts of risk very scary, very threatening to their sense of well-being. It would not take much change for them to go from Entitlement to Fear. Other people are much more comfortable with some levels of uncertainty or risk. People who put challenge high on their list of requirements for personal satisfaction are less likely to be panicked when there's a moderate increase in uncertainty. And finally, there are a small number of people who enjoy risk and who create it when their lives become too predictable.

If we were to graph the experiences of individuals within an organization, particularly an organization in significant transition, we would have separate and disjointed waves; see Figure 5-7.

Paradoxically, many organizations that are deepest into Entitlement will attract individuals who are most interested in

Figure 5-7. Anxiety amounts experienced by individuals.

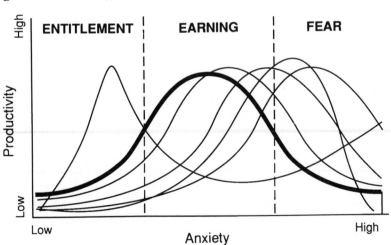

Earning. Entitled organizations include many of our most famous companies that have enormous resources and typically
pay exceedingly well. They have always attracted very bright
people, many of whom are highly motivated to achieve and
compete. I've had these employees say to me "I'm a 5. I always
look for a manager who's a 6, so I'll always have to stretch. What
really worries me, and I don't think I could handle it, is if I had
to work for a 2."

Those inner-directed, results-oriented people do not fit
into that organization's culture of Entitlement. Usually, one of
three things happens: (1) They become terribly frustrated and
leave. (2) If they stay, they will plateau early because they don't
fit in. (3) They may adapt to the institution's culture, retaining
their ambition but losing their capacity to initiate and take risks.

Once in a while we see individuals who can retain an Earning mind-set within conditions of Entitlement, but that's not
very likely if they remain within those conditions for long. If
they do manage to keep their Earning psychology, it's probably
because they have had at least some occasional real challenges
and demands for high performance within the organization, or
they are having those experiences somewhere else in their life.

When there is a large gap between the institutional and the
individual comfort level with risk (see Fig. 5-8), the best choice
is usually for the individual to leave. It's very difficult to move
an organization by yourself; it's tragic to give up an esteemed
part of yourself.

Making Changes

Let's assume that we now understand the three psychological
states and their consequences in human behaviors. With the
model, we have a tool for measuring the three conditions. Now,
how do we make use of this understanding to improve our organizations? How will we get to a psychology of Earning if we
are not there already? In a deliberate and constructive way, we
have to use risk. Looking at your organization, consider these
questions:

Figure 5-8. Misfit between the individual and the organization.

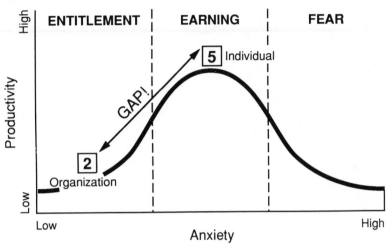

- Why should we change? What is there in the environment that creates the urgency?
- What core changes are needed? What are the biggest issues?
- Where should we start? What do we focus on? The organization? A division? An individual?
- Where are we on the curve? Which direction do we need to go in?
- What's our basic strategy for moving from one state to another? Do we know enough about the possible techniques?
- Who is in charge of the change? We'll need to identify individuals or a team with clear responsibilities.
- How will we protect the innovators of change? Do we need mechanisms for group evaluations and decisions?
- What's in it for the individual who changes?
- What happens to individuals who don't change?
- What will we tell everyone?

Assuming change is needed (the first two items), what's the process of bringing it about?

What Kind of Problem?

The first step is to be clear about what you are dealing with. Is the problem an organizational one or does it involve one or more individuals? That will tell you whether you need an organizational policy or an individual intervention.

Executives and top-level managers will probably be concerned with the entire organization as one entity. They should watch for variations within that one entity. Some people within the organization, as individuals, will fall at different points from where the organization as a whole falls. If the environment involves a merger or acquisition of organizations with different cultures, there can be differences on a very large scale.

Mid-level managers, shop supervisors, managers of work units or teams, and anyone else who is responsible for the performance of more than a few people will also probably start with a focus on the organization, although the organization in question will be much smaller (perhaps a department or work group) and individual differences may assume greater importance.

Those concerned with the performance and work attitudes of one or a few people will look toward the descriptions for individuals. Here is also where you will focus if you are wise enough to see the need for change in yourself and are brave enough to tackle it.

Which Direction?

Next to be considered is "Where are we (if this is an organizational problem) on the Earning curve?" Or, if you're focused at the individual level, "Where is this person on the curve?" Remember that your goal is to be at the midpoint, where the best work gets done. To move to that point, you may have to increase pressure or decrease it. Once you know where the organization or the individual is on the curve, you know in which direction you have to move.

As best you can, assess the current conditions using the descriptions of the nine phases. This assessment involves two tasks. You have to monitor behavior and, since the critical variable is an emotion, you must also trust how it feels. On either the organizational or the individual level, observe what people *do* and monitor how these actions *feel*. Be as exact as possible, which is seldom easy. For one thing, as we mentioned earlier, people and companies rarely fit neatly into just one category.

■ If you see lots of long hours but nothing much is achieved, if there's lots of bureaucratic caution, and if people never challenge each other, chances are good that the emotional climate is flat and apathetic. Then you're in Entitlement. (*Caution:* Where Entitlement is extreme, so is denial. In that case, outside observers are probably necessary both to assess the core state and to strategize for change.)

■ If no work is getting done because people are paralyzed by panic or preoccupied with protecting their own turf; if you sense a climate of depression, cynicism, and mistrust; and if people seem narcissistic and grasping, chances are you're in Fear.

■ If work is being produced and people are optimistic, gutsy, energetic, involved, excited, and oriented to the future, you're in Earning.

What Strategy?

Once you know in which direction to move, you can begin to plan your strategy for orchestrating change. In general terms, the overall approaches for each condition are:

■ If your assessment shows that the mood is primarily one of Entitlement, some level of tension must be constructed. That's done by creating significant positive or negative outcomes as a result of performance. For example, "If we don't hit our targets, no one gets a bonus."

■ If you determine that the mood is overly anxious, then you must take steps to reduce anxiety. Be straight about what is happening and what people can expect; don't leave any room for rumors. Emphasize successes and historic stability. Strive for calm.

▪ If you have a condition of Earning, your goal is to maintain and nurture it, with perhaps a little fine-tuning to make it even better. Your biggest danger is that you'll increase or decrease the risk level when it's not needed and take people into a less optimal part of the curve.

What Next?

In all cases, the generalized states have to be converted to specific problems or issues that lend themselves to being managed. For example, the core issues in Entitlement are often things like a weighty bureaucracy with too many rules, a culture that resists innovation, or a lack of confidence in subordinates. Those are awfully big institutional issues. More progress is likely if they can be transformed into smaller and specific tasks such as "Let's cut out levels of management, go through the manuals and cut out rules, and be sure everyone knows they can't send decisions up."

The next three chapters consider the specifics of change. For both individuals and organizations, strategies for each of the nine points on the curve are described and many specific techniques are presented. If you are in Entitlement, turn to Chapter 6. If you are in Fear, turn to Chapter 7. If you are in Earning, turn to Chapter 8.

Whenever the goal is to change the organization, it's necessary that the reasons for change be articulated very clearly. Because understanding always facilitates change, executives and managers need to tell people what they're trying to accomplish and why.

Organizational change from one set of values to another can easily take from three to five years. But taking no action will jeopardize the very survival of your organization.

6

Moving Away From Entitlement—Increase Pressure

The only way to energize lethargic organizations and people is to push them into the psychology of Earning. It usually takes some shaking up—perhaps even a crisis. But after years of avoiding risk, people find any risk frightening. It is important to remember that when there is a lot of Entitlement, any movement toward Earning, even if it is small, feels like Fear at first. That's why we say that any movement out of deep Entitlement toward Earning always means moving first into Fear. And that's precisely why it's so hard.

Naturally, people resist leaving the comfort of Entitlement. When they're pushed out of it, they will try to return. Even managers have a tendency to return to the bureaucratic security of Entitlement as soon as the latest crisis is past. This rebound effect is inevitable; people always tend to slide backward. That's why continued pressure is needed to make the changes stick.

Senior managers will need great courage and toughness. It takes courage to sustain the pressure long enough so people truly realize Entitlement is over. The period of change will inevitably be a time of low morale: Expect lots of complaining, delaying, and resisting (see Fig. 6-1, which displays the full process). Drastic measures may be called for. A new vision will not take people into Earning; more than a carrot, you will need a stick.

Figure 6-1. Using stress to create excitement.

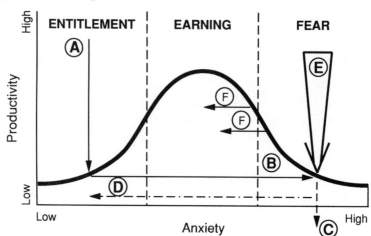

(A) Performance is required.
(B) From Entitlement to Fear.
(C) Morale plunges.
(D) Efforts are made to return to Entitlement.
(E) Despite lowered morale, requirements for performance are sustained.
(F) Only in this way do people and organizations learn that the only way to reduce anxiety is to earn your way out.

Only pressure takes people and organizations out of Entitlement. But pressure is only half the prescription; the other half is support. Apply pressure while applying support. Pressure takes the form of required achievement; support takes the form of information, counseling, and tools.

You must be careful not to exert so much pressure that people go to the extreme right of the curve, into panic. The longer people and organizations remain in the high-anxiety sector, the more fearful they will become. Then you have the opposite problem: Rather than being complacent, people are too paralyzed to work.

Three Overall Approaches

In this chapter we examine ways to counteract the conditions of Entitlement. We use two phases. First, as a kind of overview, we revisit the first three points of the Earning curve, the Entitlement section:

Point 1:	Confront with support.
Point 2:	Confront.
Point 3:	Challenge.

These strategies take slightly different forms, depending on whether the affected group is an entire organization or one or more individuals.

When it is the entire organization that needs changing, the driving force must be the top leaders. They must be prepared to maintain pressure, encourage attempts, tolerate mistakes, and reward achievements. More specifically, there are three overall strategies for organizational change, one for each of the three Entitlement points on the curve. They are summarized in the sidebar.

Entitled Organizations: What Executives Should Do

Point 1. *Confront with support.* The focus is on increasing accountability. The message to be communicated throughout the organization is "We waste too much time and energy on things that aren't important. We have to get things in focus. If we don't get more stuff out, and faster, we're in big trouble. Let's figure out what really counts."

Point 2. *Confront.* The focus is on evaluation. The message from the top should be: "Our evaluations are too high. Everyone gets graded 'outstanding,' but we have people who don't pull their weight and we have others who do the work of three. From now on everyone's going to be ranked. There's going to be no more hiding."

Point 3: *Challenge.* The organization's focus should be on *pushing power down.* The message to be communicated is

"Things are too comfortable around here. From now on we expect everyone to have an opinion and we're going to ask for it. We expect everyone to defend their point of view. We want to hear a lot more from the people who actually do the work. Managers and supervisors, you are to talk less, listen more, and require participation."

If the focus of attention is a smaller unit—even one person—the overall techniques are the same, but they show themselves in slightly different ways. For managers working with individuals, it is often a question of how best to motivate (see the sidebar).

Entitled Individuals: What Managers Should Do

Point 1. *Confront with support.* Be very clear about requiring performance and be specific. Provide a time when the job is to be completed and keep it short—no more than a week. Verbalize your availability for help. Say something like "This is exactly what I want you to do. You have two days to do it. Remember, if you have any trouble with this, I want you to come to me and I'll help. I'm here if you need me."

Point 2. *Confront.* Increase the conditionality of receiving rewards. Provide short to medium time parameters. "This is your assignment. I want it ready for my review by noon on Friday. That's four days from now. I expect to see a significant improvement in accuracy over your last two assignments. If I don't get it, you're not earning your salary."

Point 3. *Challenge.* Motivate this person by communicating an attitude of "You're capable of doing significantly better work. I'm confident you can do it. I expect much more from you." Sustain pressure. Use constructive competition. Being a member of the team has to be earned.

Using Pressure to Increase Productivity: Seven Strategies

Here are seven specific techniques for deliberately increasing the anxiety level. Although all could be used at any level in the Entitlement portion of the curve, they are particularly appropriate to one particular level, noted in the number in parentheses:

1. Increase accountability through evaluation (level 1).
2. Require ongoing risk-taking (level 1).
3. Increase visibility and peer pressure; flatten the hierarchy (level 20).
4. Increase conditionality and reward differentially (level 2).
5. Visibily fire for nonperformance (level 2).
6. Create competition (level 3).
7. Assure a meritocracy (level 3).

Remember that real situations are usually complicated, because pure types are rare. In addition, as we create change, we cannot know absolutely what the outcome will be. We can strategize and plan changes, but in reality the change that occurs may be only an approximation of our plan. Trying, fixing, and adapting are always necessary.

Many of these techniques are interconnected: Organizations may be structured in such a way that these various techniques occur in a natural flow from one to the next. That is, when you increase peer pressure, you are at the same time creating the conditions of meritocracy. When you push power down by flattening a hierarchy, you automatically increase accountability. And when you formulate a reward system that is linked to that accountability, you have increased conditionality ("You don't get the reward unless you do what we hold you accountable for") and you are also rewarding differentially (strong producers get more than weak producers.)

Whirlpool shows how strategies can be linked. CEO David Whitman says "We have a new organizational structure and have pushed accountability into that structure much more. We put in place a bonus plan which allows better monitoring of performance and provides greater incentives."

Increase Accountability Through Evaluations

People need to be held accountable for doing real work and that work must be evaluated. The accountability must be in terms of the core, or most important parts, of a person's responsibilities. That is, identify what is real work and decide how to evaluate it. Then reinforce those evaluations by tying compensation to performance. Performance must be sharply differentiated from the amount of time people work. People need to be continually asked "What value do you add?"

What Is Real Work?

The organization needs an objective and systematic review of jobs, analyzing the value of assignments and differentiating between core and peripheral tasks. This process requires that managers be clear about what really needs to be accomplished. Take the time to think through what the essential business of the company is and therefore what constitutes real work or significant added value.

Periodically all units should initiate a major review, seeking to answer: What business are we really in? What work is really important? What work (and employees) are redundant or superfluous? How excellent are we? Are we preparing for the future? Insist that all workers be directly involved in the analysis; for example, ask them: "If you had 20 percent less (or more) time, how would you change your job? If you could, how would you redesign your job?"

The purpose of this review is to determine what people (or the unit) should focus on and be held most accountable for. We have to discriminate between putting in time and achieving something significant. Being busy is not the same as being productive. Creating mountains of elegant paper is not the same as adding value. Measure people's performance—what they actually contribute. This measurement will require clear, attainable, and worthwhile goals.

In 1990, Oryx, a Texas oil and gas producer, saved $70 million by getting rid of procedures, reviews, reports, and approvals that had little to do with discovering oil, which is the company's *real* work. Three years earlier, after dropping 1,500 positions, Oryx found its costs were still too high. A consulting firm surveyed the remaining employees and discovered they were concentrating mostly on meeting budget targets, not on locating oil.

Oryx set up teams of employees from all departments to identify unnecessary work. Following the teams' recommendations, the company discontinued 25 percent of all internal reports, decided that four signatures on requests for capital expenditures were enough (not twenty), and found ways to produce the annual budget in six weeks instead of seven months. Over the next two years, Oryx cut another 1,500 jobs, mostly middle managers whose work had largely been eliminated. Now the company is replacing its oil reserves twice as fast at half the cost.

As the Oryx experience demonstrates, the tough examination of job content is especially important when some downsizing has occurred. Many companies have cut so they have a leaner structure, but after they downsized, they didn't reduce the work load. You have to constantly look at people's work and ask "Is this necessary? Is it important to the mission? To the customer?" You have to prioritize. You probably need to relearn that great word, "No." Cut paper work; don't document things to death. Eliminate work that doesn't really contribute and get people to do the critical tasks. Work should emphasize what must be done, not what would be nice to have.

Start evaluating the content of jobs in parts of the organization where discontent is high and satisfaction is low. People there may already be motivated to get things improved.

Evaluating Real Performance

There are several ways to make it easier to evaluate others and then communicate the evaluation. One is to use teams of evaluators. Individuals may feel uncomfortable judging others, but the pooled evaluation of several judges can be communicated with more confidence and greater impersonality than the estimate of one person. In this instance, procedures can be of great help. In many institutions, individual evaluations are the simultaneous responsibility of several people.

The organization should gather evaluations about people's performance from a range of superiors, peers, and subordinates regularly (e.g., every four to six months). Sometimes these evaluations are anonymous; this decision is up to company policy.

Since evaluations are usually skewed too positively, people who communicate evaluations need support in order to become more honest about negative input. That support can be created by having evaluation data from a range of other people, or having evaluations be the result of a consensus from a number of judges. That is, evaluation boards can be created and summary evaluations can be communicated by someone other than an individual's own manager.

Also, the evaluation procedure can be more comfortable for the evaluator if very detailed judgments are not required. When the range of ability is so narrow that people are very similar to each other, use only a few categories of performance. Pushing fine distinctions when people have comparable abilities is difficult for the evaluators and demoralizing for the workers.

Many tasks are not easily quantified. In those cases, consider evaluation procedures that involve using several experts to evaluate the work performance. Together, they present their opinions to the person's manager. This group approach means that those making the assessment are also being judged, and therefore people in this situation tend to be careful and thoughtful in their evaluations.

Institute evaluation by peers and subordinates as well as by superiors. It's harder to impress a group of people than one person. Impressing a group tends to require performance; flattery won't help much. Also, the judgments of a group are harder to dismiss than the idiosyncrasies of an individual. Customer evaluations can be an additional source of pressure for accountability and an additional kind of information for determining compensation.

Reinforcing Real Performance Through Rewards

Accountability and the reward system must be intertwined. People need to have some of their rewards at risk in the sense that the reward can be gained only when they meet the specific and most important goals they are accountable for achieving. (The idea of differentiating rewards according to performance is discussed later in this chapter as a strategy in the section "Reward Differentially, Increase Conditionally.") Work will be organized in small groups in order to increase peer pressure (see strategy discussed in the section, "Increase Visibility and Peer Pressure"), but the largest percentage of the evaluation should be based on the group's performance (65 percent); the individual's performance should be a smaller portion (35 percent).

It is likely that pressure will have to be built into the evaluation system. Pressure has to bear on poor performers, so that if they remain poor performers, it will be uncomfortable for them and hard for them to stay in the company. Poor performers rarely improve, especially once they've developed an attitude of Entitlement, unless there are real consequences to performing or not.

The organization might start by using forced ranking with clearly different rewards for those at different percentiles. If that isn't enough pressure, if the organization is deep into Entitlement, clear and negative outcomes are required. For example, the bottom 5 percent could be put on probation; the bottom 6 to 15 percent would get neither a merit nor a cost of living salary increase. A forced distribution could be created in which only 5 percent can be exceptional, 25 percent are outstanding, 40 percent are average, 25 percent meet requirements, and 5 percent must be graded as unsatisfactory.

Require Ongoing Risk Taking

Since Entitlement is the result of too little risk, organizations should require that people experience challenge on an ongoing basis, even without a job change. People are not allowed to become or remain narrow experts nor are they permitted to become complacent, because new assignments require learning and risk taking.

Create opportunities for work challenge. Create an organizational policy of releasing people for new assignments. Stimulate more rotation assignments between line and staff. Unless the circumstances of the work, or the content of the responsibilities, or the interactions within the assignment are changing, no one should be allowed to continue doing the same work for more than three years because the most complex job is mastered within that time. An appropriate target is that every year, about 25 percent of people's assignments should be new to them.

At Toronto Dominion Bank, top management has decreed that the "new" bank will be a place where people will not be punished for taking risks. "What you should do," they are saying, "is actively look around this organization for opportunities to take on bigger responsibilities to make your job more exciting. Innovate. Do it!"

Policies should operate from the premise that people want the chance to meet challenge, master new skills, work through risks, innovate, make a difference, and lead. These policies have to become a working assumption, with the result that people take change for granted and view those who resist job change as deficient.

The definition of success will have to include the idea of earning different and sometimes more difficult assignments, with increasing levels of autonomy and decision-making responsibilities. Management should assume people can be largely responsible for themselves, can analyze and make decisions, and can initiate.

Increase Visibility and Peer Pressure

The key is to make people visible and you do that by flattening the hierarchy. People hide in the bureaucracy by handing decisions up, by creating committees. With a leaner and flatter structure, everyone is more visible. There aren't layers within which to hide.

Whenever possible, work should be assigned to small groups of people of similar status. The performance of the entire group will be evaluated, not the individual; this will increase the power of peer pressure to perform. It will also increase the bonding within the group, thus providing emotional support.

Though a flatter organization would appear to have fewer bosses and therefore less pressure to perform, people can be held responsible more easily when there's less of a hierarchy because it's harder to pass things on. In a flat organization, especially if the unit is a demarcated team with responsibility to produce, there'll be a lot of peer pressure on every individual to contribute, perform, and produce. It's much easier to hide from one boss than it is to be invisible to eight peers.

Peer pressure may be vastly more effective than any other kind. Peers can exert the pressure of accountability at the same time they support individuals.

Although performance is measured, for most people it's not necessary in terms of motivating them to perform. People feel responsible for achieving whatever their responsibilities are, partly because they know they'll be held accountable, but largely because they're in a milieu where people are unwilling to waste their time shuffling paper and evading responsibilities. People are willing to work very hard; they are not willing to have others around who don't.

While management monitors and evaluates performance, most of the work is handed off to reasonably autonomous teams composed of people of similar rank. Visibility and accountability are easier to achieve when units are made small. Organize so as to increase functional collaboration and mutual responsibility while keeping operating units small enough that players and their performance are visible to others. Nissan, for example, boasts of having the best attendance record in the United States, and that's without time clocks. It helps that Nissan's people are organized into teams of about twenty, so absentees are swiftly noticed. It further helps that Japanese plants are organized without relief workers. When someone's not present, the rest of the team members are supposed to pick up the slack.

Effective teams require input about decisions from everyone. Many groups are cross-functional or cross-skill teams, composed of people with a range of experiences and assumptions. For example, a new product design team could include people from engineering, manufacturing, sales, market research, and package design. In team meetings, all members simultaneously suggest issues from their own points of view. Their goal is to anticipate from the very beginning issues that could be important. This is in strong contrast to the traditional way of doing things, where engineering would design a product that manufacturing would then build with different specifications, and sales would be stuck trying to market a product that was different from what customers had been promised.

When the Honda Accord was being developed, the project manager held early brainstorming sessions with about a hundred people from many parts of the organization. Then, in line with Honda's tradition, these people developed two competing concepts of what the car might be like.

One important aspect of good teams is that they tend to foster innovative thinking. While all team members are expected to work cooperatively, it is also presumed that they will defend their divergent perspectives. I call it creative confrontation. It requires that people feel comfortable in disagreeing and that disagreement is not hostile. The objective is to develop superior solutions, which is most easily done in teams or task forces of peers who are cooperatively engaged and responsible.

Reward Differentially, Increase Conditionally

In most of our organizations, traditionally every job was classified and assigned a pay value. Despite the elaborate evaluation systems, there was little real variability in pay as a reflection of job performance. In these traditional systems, people get raises more or less automatically, either across the board (everyone gets a 6 percent increase every year) or when they move into a certain level of seniority (this is especially predominant in entitled organizations).

The situation is changing; people are beginning to be paid for contribution, not status. People come to realize that they can directly influence their rewards by how much they contribute. Those who make a greater contribution earn more and seniority has nothing to do with it.

People need to feel that they have an impact on what happens to them. That's why increasing numbers of companies are giving employees full financial information and saying "If we are profitable, you get a bonus." Rewards are possible, but there are conditions to be met.

The president of a general contracting firm opened the books to her seventy-two employees. Then she said "There will be no more raises. The only way people will be able to increase their money is by earning a bonus. Bonuses will depend on whether we're profitable." In addition to increased productivity, there was a marked decrease in costs. Before, no one had given any thought to calling long-distance during peak hours. Over time, the group became its own cost-cutting overseer.

Incentive Pay Plans

Incentive pay is critical. Without incentives for productivity, performance tends to slacken. Very simply, some amount of pay must be at risk when people are too comfortable.

Of course, there are many kinds of rewards, not all of them financial. Being a member of the winning team or being publicly recognized are extremely important rewards, but money is the most obvious. People may have difficulty in perceiving the reward value of varying opportunities to lead or make decisions, but they instantly perceive the difference between $5 and $500. Thus, some amount of money should be at risk.

Driven by increased competition and the need to improve performance, more and more organizations are increasing the variable component of pay. About 75 percent of American employers now have at least one kind of incentive pay plan and the great majority were installed after the 1981–82 recession when the permanent need to cut costs and increase productivity became clear.

The plans are not just for middle managers. At Borden, for example, some 28,000 workers at 180 different plants in 1990 had the chance to win bonuses ranging from $250 to $800 each, depending on how well their individual plants met various attendance, safety, quality, production, and financial goals.

Some of the plans affect more than bonuses: Some portion of the base salary is also at risk. At Saturn, GM's new subsidiary, salaries are 80 percent of normal union scale; the rest is earned if workers reach productivity targets. If they do better than the targets, they earn more than 100 percent of their salary.

Monsanto has twenty-one different incentive plans, and thirteen of them link scheduled raises to performance. If they meet established goals, workers get the raise that is scheduled; if they exceed their goals, they get extra cash. "We used to focus on pay to attract, retain, and motivate," says Barry Bingham, Monsanto's corporate compensation director. "Now, we're using pay as a tool to drive results."

Planning Your Strategy

▪ *Involve employees in designing the program.* There is good evidence that the new pay systems do raise productivity. The effect may be greater when the organization has a significant amount of employee participation in decision making and employees have more responsibility and autonomy.

Greater involvement on the part of employees is almost certain to engender greater acceptance of the system. If the criteria of performance are obviously appropriate, and those making the evaluations are obviously credentialed, those who are judged as underproductive are likely to accept the evaluation. Equally important, employees are usually very angry when the reward system doesn't reflect differences in performance. High performers are bitter about the lack of demonstrated appreciation for them and the fact that they're carrying underproductive people.

Organizations have to be careful to link the largest sector of the pay at risk with outcomes in which people are involved, responsible, and control. For example, a team bonus should be based on what the team achieved and not on the profitability of the entire organization.

▪ *Include the entire organization, top to bottom.* Nonmanagement employees are not the only ones who have to have rewards at risk. Management at all levels must be part of the system too. Incentive pay is based on the notion that everyone's in the same boat. When anxiety and mistrust are high, it does not help that incentive pay is at risk in the ranks but the pay of CEOs bears little or no relation to company performance. The lack of a relationship is especially demoralizing when business is declining. When executives are exempt from the accountability that is imposed on everyone else, mistrust and bitterness are increased exponentially.

- *Be prepared for initial resistance.* Where the system fostered Entitlement, any introduction of money at risk will be reacted to very negatively at first. A few years ago one of the regional Bell companies introduced a system of risk and bonuses. It set salaries at the seventy-fifth percentile of what the market was paying. Then management said "80 percent of your salary is a given; the other 20 percent is at risk. You may make more than the 20 percent if you are very productive and if we are profitable." Even though in the two years the system had operated people made more than the 20 percent in bonuses, they grumbled. And that was good: Management had to get their attention; it needed to communicate that the days of Entitlement were gone.

- *Include punishment as well as reward.* Everyone has to know that failure to achieve has consequences. There has to be a real response to performance. In addition to the possibility of gaining rewards, there also has to be the possibility of some kind of punishment. Punishment may involve not getting bonuses or raises. It may be nonfinancial such as not being selected to participate in a leadership course. Whenever rewards are available, not getting can have more impact than getting. The range of punishment should also include something stronger such as being demoted or fired (see the strategy discussed in the next section, "Fire for Nonperformance").

- *Assess your situation.* The need for differential rewards is clear, but there is a special case where rewards should not be differential: Whenever performance of individuals is roughly equal, imposing differentials is demotivating. In teams of highly skilled professionals selected for certain technical expertise, for instance, we would expect them all to be at approximately the same level of excellence. Surprisingly, however, using differentials is a fairly common practice in companies that use teams of highly selected professionals, because it is assumed that without that pressure, there will be little motivation to perform. Since professionals are usually highly motivated to begin with, this is really the imposition of a demotivating punishment.

Fire for Nonperformance

Where Entitlement has a long history, people resist increases in pressure by denying that anything has changed. In the face of risk, they will hang on to Entitlement with the fiercest of embraces. It's necessary to get their attention, possibly by firing employees who don't perform.

I am not suggesting that firing be used arbitrarily. Those who are separated must clearly be underachieving and must have had an opportunity to increase their performance as a result of evaluation, guidance, and appropriate support. Then, if performance does not improve adequately, people should be fired.

In organizations of historic Entitlement, it will be a significant change in practice if not in policy. Those organizations usually have procedures by which people can be involuntarily separated from employment, but the procedures take endless time and endless paper.

The strategy here is to make it known throughout the organization that firing is indeed an option. Don't continue old euphemisms such as "decided to leave for personal reasons." Go public with the truth. Out of respect, don't use names, but include in periodic status reports a statement such as "Seven people left for regular retirement, twenty-three took early retirement, four left to other organizations, and six people were fired for inadequate performance."

Create Competition

The strategy here is to make competition continuous and important. People need to measure how they're doing all the time.

It's especially useful to have an outside competitor, a villain to wage war against. If no outside villain is available, people may have to compete against their previous levels of performance, as their goals are raised; or the competition can be against other individuals, teams, units, or institutions.

Create a race against your competitive adversaries and keep score. Square D, which manufactures electrical equipment, put up a scoreboard on the outside wall of its headquarters building. Every day the board displays quarterly financial data: profit per employee, sales per employee, and return on equity for Square D compared to its main competitors—Emerson Electric, General Electric, and Westinghouse.

Personalizing an adversary can be energizing—the relationship between Coke and Pepsi springs to mind. As long as people are in the competition, it should be exciting and exhilarating. When employees are fighting against a common enemy, strong bonding occurs. Later, they will recall the years when they were competing for survival as the time when they had the most fun.

Keep raising your goals. As soon as you're near reaching the old goals, create big, new ones. Set performance targets that are stretch goals, but that 90 percent of the people will make. Then, the competition to reach the new goals is initially an enforced pressure for higher performance. As the goals are reached, the success is a positive experience.

Competition can be used to jar people out of Entitlement, especially when it's tied to differential rewards. We do not want to create a situation where a few people win and everyone else loses. The end point of the competition has to be a psychology of Earning and a sense of winning.

Create a Meritocracy

In a meritocracy, people at different levels of status, with different skills, styles, and backgrounds, can all earn the right to participate, influence, decide, lead, and succeed. All workers, at whatever hierarchical level, have an opportunity to demonstrate what they can do. Skill counts; status does not.

In a meritocracy, market forces prevail, in the sense that there is a continuous internal competition for increasing amounts of different kinds of power; one's hierarchical position is no protection from others' abilities and skills.

The idea is to create a culture in which subordinates expect to earn increasing decision-making power or autonomy and managers expect to delegate. This involves upward pressure from subordinates who presume their right to earn autonomy. The organizational caste system has to open to become a family of people who earned their entrance or their belonging.

The goal is the development of many leaders with a range of styles. Challenge by developing an organizational culture that makes it clear that "What's my job?" is the wrong question. People are continuously asked to instead answer "What's my function? What is the purpose of what I am doing? With that in mind, is there a better approach?"

Meritocracies enable the kind of creative confrontation we talked about earlier in this chapter. Searching, questioning, dissent, even conflict are givens. The confrontation may be heated, but it is not personal: There is too much respect for other people's abilities. Management must elicit opinions and then allow the differences to illuminate or lead to understanding. Executives and managers need to be trained to both collaborate and creatively confront employees in impersonal discussions so they model the behavior the organization wants.

Everyone, at all levels, should have opportunities for training, access to new positions, and participation in meetings, project teams, and the like. Management will be trained to ask and listen, as well as to tell and order. They should be trained to empower or delegate, to measure outcome, to involve subordinates in a bottom-up communication of recommendations for improvement, and to delegate to teams of peers. Leaders are expected to emerge from within the team.

A significant reward for excellence of input will be that the ideas get implemented. Publicize people at all hierarchical levels who initiated some new ideas, who took appropriate risks.

7

Moving Away From Fear— Decrease Pressure

We have talked a lot about the disabling condition called Entitlement, but the opposite condition is just as debilitating. Fear, particularly at the extreme end of the curve where it becomes paralysis, destroys creative energy just as surely as the lethargy of Entitlement. Fear, anxiety, uncertainty mean the same thing: deep-down panic that your job is in jeopardy and the situation is out of your control.

To get back on track, organizations must first reduce anxiety by creating mechanisms by which people can earn reasonable levels of security. The parameters of what can be earned, the nature of the contract, and mutual expectations and requirements should be spelled out. People need to know what's being required and what they can expect.

Very simply, uncertainty is reduced when people are told what's going on and what will happen to them. In the vacuum of no news, employees imagine the worst. Since disappointment is much easier to handle than anxiety, honesty is the best policy.

The organization has to experience forward momentum, which requires that managers give employees short-term goals that are definitely and swiftly achievable, and executives create long-term wins. Employees need to know where they're heading, what's happening, and what strategies have been designed to get them there. As accomplishments are achieved, they must be loudly publicized and those who achieved them have to be visibly rewarded.

General Approaches

As with Entitlement, there are generalized strategies for each of the three Fear points on the Earning curve.

Point 9:	Support by addressing emotion.
Point 8:	Support through success and by addressing emotion.
Point 7:	Support through success.

The strategies take a slightly different focus on the organizational level than on the individual level (see sidebars).

When designing an intervention strategy it's important to assess how the state of Fear emerged. Was it a sudden shift caused by external forces (a hostile takeover)? Or was it a deliberate push away from years of Entitlement? We need to remember that where there's been a long period of Entitlement, anxiety has to be increased and maintained long enough for employees to believe it's a new ball game. Thus, if you're concerned with companies or individuals who are in the sector of Fear, especially in 7 or 8, because they've been forced out of Entitlement, then you must sustain pressure despite their discomfort with the high anxiety level. Only if they're at 9 should pressure be reduced.

On the other hand, if there's been a long period of very high anxiety, people need relief. It's conceivable that even more than experiences of success or triumph, they need a period of calm, in which things are stable and predictable and nothing much happens.

Organizations in Fear: What Leaders Must Do

Point 9. *Support by addressing emotion.* Executives need to project a sense that they know what is happening, they know how people feel, they care, and they want to help. Over and over, they need to communicate "It's better than it looks. We will be fine. It will be okay. In fact, it's going to be better than okay."

Point 8. *Support through success and by addressing emotion.* In this organization the major emphasis must be on the progress that surely is ahead as everyone works together. The message of progress must be simple and consistent: "We know it's been tough, but it's going to be better. More clearly than ever, we know what our real business is. Now we're in a much better position than ever to invest in our success. It will take time, but we're making it happen."

Point 7. *Support through success.* Emphasize the opportunities that lie in the future. Stress the organization's movements toward greater success and explain how individuals can contribute and participate in it.

Individuals in Fear: What Managers Must Do

Point 9. *Support by addressing emotion.* People at 9 can't reduce anxiety through their own performance; the reassurance and support must be provided by others. Thus, managers need to be accessible and approachable. Let employees know that you understand how they are feeling. The message is "It's okay to feel the way you do. You're not alone in feeling that way. I am ready to help. It looks bad now, but it's really better than you think. And it's going to be a whole lot better. You're going to be fine."

Point 8. *Support through success and by addressing emotion.* People at 8 also need their emotional state to be acknowledged, but they need the anxiety-reducing experience of success as well. Maintain some amount of pressure, but keep the time frame short. Emphasize the idea that together, everyone will succeed. Recognize achievements, demonstrating that success is possible.

Managers could say "I know how you're feeling. It's hard right now, but if we pull together and work hard, it's going to be just fine. Here's exactly what to do. Get on the team. I know you're wondering what's going to happen, but it's going to get better, you'll see."

Point 7. *Support through success.* Provide goals (or require the individual to develop them) that involve opportunities to make decisions, learn new material, and meet some form of challenge. Success will breed confidence and confidence reduces anxiety. The attitude to communicate is "Here's a chance to show what you can do. I'm confident you can succeed."

In this chapter you will learn some specific strategies for adjusting the organizational temperature back toward the mid-range of Earning. The strategies would work for all stages of Fear, but some are better for certain levels than others (check the numbers in parentheses in the list below). Once again, remember that seldom is an organization or an individual a perfect fit for any one level. Remember, too, that change has a way of twisting on you; the eventual outcome of your interventions may not exactly match your plan. In that case, take another assessment and start on a new course.

Here are suggested ways to lower anxiety levels:

Reducing Pressure: Nine Strategies

1. Make leadership visible (level 9).
2. Communicate concern for the individual (level 9).
3. Create trust in the organization (level 9).
4. Publicize achievements and restore confidence (level 8).
5. Provide information (level 8).
6. Make it possible for people to earn security and belonging (level 8).
7. Create procedures to enforce fairness (level 8).
8. Communicate goals and plans (level 8).
9. Reduce the emphasis on hierarchy (level 7).

Make Leadership Visible

When anxiety is high, so are dependency needs. Employees are looking to the leaders to give them faith that the future will be better. They are vulnerable and want to believe they can depend on those in command. That's why trust becomes especially important.

To maintain trust, leadership must be consistent. Credibility is lost when there are big discrepancies between what leaders say and what they do. In the wake of downsizing in the 1980s, there was a decrease in the perception that management practices what it preaches. Increasing credibility requires openness. Hidden agendas will destroy trust.

When uncertainty is high, leadership has to project certainty and confidence. People desperately need to believe that the leaders know what they are doing. Leaders must appear thoughtful, decisive, wise, and considerate. Management needs to increase its perceived trustworthiness, dedication, sagacity, and shrewdness.

Decisions sometimes must be made before you have all the information. It's what Barry Gibbons, CEO of Burger King, calls the theory of vacuum management. He says "When you make a major change, you create a kind of corporate vacuum while employees wait to see what happens. The trick is to fill that vacuum with positive ideas before others fill it with negative ones. This means telling people what's happening, what you're going to do."

Leadership must be very visible, both in person and through all the institutional media such as newsletters, magazines, and internal videotapes. Increase approachability; people want the sense that they can gain access to management. Practice management by walking around and encourage managers and top professionals to do the same. Get out of the office—literally. Be seen talking to people. Have lunch in the company cafeteria; stop and talk to people there. What you're doing is modeling approachability.

Use all opportunities to talk informally about what you plan to do, but don't be drawn into defensive arguing when employees complain. Especially if your organization is at 9, you'll need patience in dealing with behaviors that are unproductive and irritating but are hard to change: clinging to the past, rigidly hanging on to rules, denying changes in the organization's competitive position, and expressing contempt for management.

Communicate Concern for the Individual

In times of high anxiety, people want to feel that management cares about them personally and appreciates the efforts they're making. Employees need to believe that leadership understands how they feel and why, and is trying to help. Thus, leaders need to treat employees with as much kindness and generosity as possible.

Management needs to be especially thoughtful about communicating appreciation. Being personally thanked for your contribution is important at any time, but especially when stress is very high. Simultaneously, executives and managers need to acknowledge the high levels of uncertainty that are prevalent. That is, they need to thank employees for their loyalty and their work under difficult circumstances.

If the company is facing the need to restructure, demonstrate compassion for employees. Wherever possible, try to retain employees by retraining them or relocating them. If you do downsize, be as constructive as possible to those who must leave. As many forms of help as can be arranged should be offered and publicized, ranging from personal counseling to career counseling to financial advice.

Outplacement services are a way of acknowledging the recipient's contribution to the organization. For survivors of downsizing, stress is high and morale is low. Besides survivor guilt, employees worry about whether they'll be next. It's become clear that providing outplacement services is as useful to those who remain as those who are let go because survivors feel that it reflects the organization's conscience and concern.

Leadership needs to communicate an understanding of the stress that people are under and a commitment to help relieve it. Some form of attention akin to therapy may need to be made available to survivors, ranging from off-site individual or group counseling to group recreational activities.

If leadership is willing to act on the suggestions or complaints of employees, it should create mechanisms to gain that upward communication. Suggestions that will not be heard or taken should not be encouraged since they will only increase employees' sense of powerlessness and cynicism.

Create Trust in the Organization

In uncertain times, employees want to find strength in the institution. They want the sense that they are a part of something larger and stronger than themselves. They want to feel that it makes sense to commit to the organization because it will endure. Therefore, executives must emphasize and communicate the strength and endurance of the organization and its long-term commitment to maximizing the well-being of its members. They need to publicize the organization's history of overcoming problems and its legacy of breakthroughs.

While under terrible pressure to reduce uncertainty and generate the security of determined goals and rules, the executives must give the organization time to develop answers to the questions: "What is our business? What do we stand for?" The temptation for executives will be to latch on to some simple solutions that are currently chic. There are no simple solutions to complex issues. A new culture of values and goals and a set of procedures cannot be bought like a new suit. Consultants and academics can be used to facilitate or accelerate the rate of change, but developing a new culture takes time, because it must reflect the truth of what is important to that organization.

Trust is increased when leadership identifies and addresses any specific discrepancies between management statements and actions. During transitions there will be unavoidable discrepancies that need to be openly discussed.

Management must also be careful to minimize gestures that imply that the organization is shaky. When there's too much change and uncertainty, people attach a lot of importance to things that are, objectively speaking, minor. Be careful of little things that can become big symbols. People in one organization compiled a list of "take-aways," things that cost very little but that management had withdrawn in the period of crisis: Christmas parties, personalized notepads, spouses being invited to company functions, and magazine subscriptions. The removal of those inexpensive items broadcast "Woe is us!" more vividly than any headline in *The Wall Street Journal*. Those symbolic acts were the clincher and many employees left.

Publicize Achievements and Restore Confidence

In the face of high anxiety, people need a sense that the organization is successfully coping with something before they can tackle larger problems. Therefore, any increments of problem solving must be publicized and the people who accomplished goals must be heralded. Reward contributions visibly and significantly. Publicize progress and breakthroughs frequently and enthusiastically, including rewarding risk-taking attempts that have not yet shown success. Visibly praise the kinds of behavior or achievements that are desired such as making decisions, initiating changes, and thinking big.

Reinforce the message "You're such a select and outstanding group (or individual) that we expect you to succeed." Teach managers that employees typically perform at the levels expected of them.

It's much easier to achieve and gain confidence when the focus of efforts is external. Therefore, make efforts to focus energy on beating the competition; as much as possible, make it a game.

Provide Information

When they feel extremely anxious about their personal future, people are skeptical and critical. They'll be skeptical that they're being told the truth and critical of those who withhold it. Thus, the strategy has to be, good news or bad, tell the truth. People need to know what to expect. It is much easier to handle bad news than free-floating anxiety. Even bad news is better than no news. When their anxiety has been tempered, people can cope with bad news by problem solving.

When you tell the truth you increase people's sense of trust even if the news is bad. When anxiety is high and there's no real information, rumors multiply. And if people discover they've been lied to, rumors multiply even faster. Once the rumors start, they have a life cycle of their own. It becomes harder and harder to kill them.

In a period of high anxiety, very little appears logical and rational. Leadership must articulate why decisions were appropriate and how they will serve to improve conditions. The rational reasons for the changes need to be spelled out and communicated over and over. In fact, you have to overcommunicate, because when anxiety is high, people don't hear.

If the anxiety is high because of a change in focus or strategy, employees should be given the results of the changes, both negative (which they probably already know) and positive, as specifically as possible. If the changes had quantitative outcomes, provide numeric data. If the changes involved a broad perspective, such as a change in organizational philosophy, values, or culture, explain the justification for the changes. New policies have to be perceived as appropriate. Discontent, criticism, and a lack of faith or trust in leadership may be reduced by providing the rationale for change from the leaders' point of view.

Employees are better able to sustain high levels of anxiety if they feel confident that the period of turbulence is finite. If possible, tell people how long the transition and resulting turbulence are expected to take.

At the individual level, and for the same reasons, managers must tell the truth about how someone is regarded. In all manner of performance evaluations, managers must learn how to communicate the truth as they see it.

Because information is so important, managers need to know whether they're getting through. They may need to create mechanisms, such as internal questionnaires and surveys, to learn whether employees received and understood communications.

Make It Possible for People to Earn Security and Belonging

Employees have a right and a need to know what kind of job security they can earn, and what they have to do to earn it. It's all right to make security conditional, if the real contract is made overt and clear. People can handle the fact that they don't have absolute job security more easily than they can deal with the anxiety of not knowing what the contract really says.

- *Articulate your expectations.* Be clear about what is considered ideal behavior. Transmit that information in multiple ways, including training programs that cover risk taking, team behavior, creativity, and the like, especially for supervisors and managers. People who are models of those behaviors should be pointed out as examples.

Managers need to articulate the most important parts of employees' assignments so they know what to focus on. Ideally, descriptions of responsibilities are jointly developed by employees and their managers as a result of normal procedures, giving employees opportunities to have input into their assignments and ensuring that they're clear about what is expected.

- *Give everyone the chance to be a winner.* When the level of stress is already very high, it's a bad idea to increase competition. Under Fear conditions, techniques like forced ranking, where people are individually graded in comparison with others, or normalized distributions in which the number of A's or C's is determined by a bell-shaped curve, should not be used. Instead, leadership should create mechanisms by which everyone has the opportunity to succeed and win. IBM's 100 percent club is an example. While winning has to be earned by filling 100 percent of a quota, there are not limits on how many people can achieve or exceed their target.

- *Provide educational tools.* People need to be given the tools with which they can deal with issues and master their responsibilities. When changes in the marketplace engender change in the organization, and people feel their jobs are at risk, providing training in new skill areas is a very real lifeline and a very tangible way for companies to help reduce Fear. Also, when change is in the air, employees need help in becoming what the new organization will want.

Therefore, organizations need to create and encourage the use of educational opportunities related both to work and to personal growth. In addition to specific skill training, the organization must provide the education that will enable everyone to understand the reasons for change.

The computerization of work, in addition to other factors, is making workers obsolete at faster and faster rates. Job-related education subsidized by the organization is essential. It may be in the form of reimbursement of tuition at higher education institutions or it may include in-house workshops and classes.

Happily, many companies are making a serious investment in employee education. Business organizations have become the largest clients of two-year community and technical colleges around the country. Millions of production line workers are going to night school classes and almost two out of five workers under age thirty-five have some college training. A report by the Carnegie Foundation in 1985 found that between 80 and 90 percent of all U.S. corporations are offering tuition reimbursement, usually for job-related courses but sometimes for any class; some are even giving time off to go to school.

- *Avoid layoffs whenever possible.* If at all possible, when anxiety levels are very high, management should try to find alternatives to layoffs, especially with experienced people. Alternatives include exploring opportunities within the company; work-sharing where several employees work part-time; or lending an executive to a nonprofit institution like the Red Cross or a government agency on a shared salary basis.

- *Build a team environment.* In addition to some kind of job security (within reasonable parameters), people need to be able to earn the security of belonging, of being a member of the team or the family. Strive for an environment where interactions should be seen as cooperative and collaborative, not competitive. Life should not be seen as a zero-sum game where if one person wins another must lose. Instead, sharing resources and knowledge should be seen as a way by which everyone can increase their chances of success.

Encourage a sense of being a member of a team by diminishing competition within the group, by focusing energy outward to competitors, by creating mechanisms of identification as team members, and by rewarding team performance.

Create Procedures to Enforce Fairness

When anxiety is very high, people want the sense that they're protected from idiosyncratic behavior or prejudiced attitudes on the part of those who control what happens to them. They want the protection of fairness built into the system. That's clearest in terms of performance evaluations, compensation, and selection for promotion.

In many organizations, evaluation, selection, and pay are controlled by one person, an employee's boss. Under ordinary circumstances, that may be adequate. When anxiety levels are high, it's not. It doesn't create any sense of protection, of institutionalized equity.

That sense of fairness is best achieved when those decisions are made by a group of people who have clearly earned their position and the right to judge others. Also, the evaluation process should be one in which several judges are responsible for evaluating an employee. Each judge must state his or her opinion to the entire group. In that sense, within the group, evaluations are public. Also, the evaluators are themselves being evaluated by their peers. This shared, public process is especially valuable in evaluating work that is not quantifiable.

Communicate Goals and Plans

Leaders have to create the perception that they have some significant control over the present and the future of the organization because they know where the organization can and should go. In terrible circumstances, strategies for survival are adequate, but planning for victory is much more powerful.

Write a description of the values and culture of the organization in the future. Create a sense of that future by continuously communicating goals and the progress being made toward them. Create a sense of the individual's future by articulating the kinds of opportunities there will be in the future. If possible, tell people what the organization will be like and how their jobs will be affected. Cast it as something positive that people can work toward.

The emphasis should be on consistency of purpose and focus. Keep as long a time frame as possible in order to generate the perception of consistency. Goals, procedures, and rules should be kept as simple and flexible as possible so there's not much need for change, which adds to the perception of consistency. Decrease ambiguity, stress, and confusion.

Don't change the focus, goals, or strategy too often. You don't want people saying "Three years ago it was teamwork, next it was quality, then it was profit margins, and this year it's empowerment. I don't know what's really important anymore. I don't know on what basis I'm being judged."

Transform general goals into very concrete ones. Create specific targets, identify specific competitors, and create a concrete way of measuring performance. Provide unit or team goal statements, including "where we are, where we were, and where we're going now."

Regularly, let work units and individuals know how things are going. For work units or the organization as a whole, construct measurements of progress and broadcast the results. For individuals, institute measurements of achievement to reinforce people's experience that they're moving toward the target and to give them greater confidence that they will be able to succeed in the new conditions.

Goals or changes must be articulated simply, explicitly, and frequently. Every means of communication should be used with lots of examples. For instance:

> Our goal in shipping is to please our customer. We used to count how many containers went out the door. That didn't let us know whether or not the customer's needs were served. Now we're counting how many did or didn't arrive within the time we promised. We're counting how many did or didn't arrive in

excellent condition. If you look at the new forms you
will see how we are measuring the quality of our deliv-
eries. You will also see that each container now has a
postcard stapled to the shipping label asking the customer to tell us how we did.

There is a hard balance here: Time must be given to develop goals and strategies while there has to be time pressure
so people can't evade their responsibility to make decisions.
With high anxiety, it's easy to evade decisions and commitments. As swiftly as possible, executives need to decide and
then communicate what business are we in, what's our general
strategy, what is each individual's piece, and what are the rules.
People need to know exactly what they're supposed to do.

Reduce the Emphasis on Hierarchy

Anxiety is reduced when people have opportunities to earn
greater confidence. They gain that confidence and a sense of
having control over their lives when others are willing to acknowledge and respond to their knowledge, skill, competence,
and experience whatever their formal status is. Thus, paradoxically, one of the best stratagems for easing stress is also one of
the best for increasing it: Reduce the emphasis on hierarchy.

Employees at all levels need experiences of problem solving, decision making, and making a difference so they have
some control over what's happening. Diminish the focus on pay
grades. Don't permit descriptions like "He couldn't do that; he's
a GS 5. We need a 7."

Give everyone opportunities to be a leader. The basic message has to be that despite tough times now, in the future there
will be opportunities to be a winner. Teach people how to "grow
their own job," or empower themselves. Leadership has to
model empowerment through "handing-off" decision-making
power. People have to know the limits of their autonomy or the
parameters within which they are free to initiate and decide.
Encourage risk taking by creating procedures by which managers "sign off" on a risky decision.

When people higher in nominal authority hand power to people lower down, by giving them the opportunity to initiate, to participate, and to decide, they are communicating respect for those people. Thus, in the long run, empowering people may be the most significant way to reduce anxiety.

We are entering an era of empowering employees. The role of manager and supervisor is changing from authority to facilitator. While the shift may require a lot of effort, the long-term benefits will include less passivity, a greater sense of personal power, more genuine teams that interact and stimulate creative performance, more honest interactions, and greater productivity.

8

Maintaining the Creative Energy of Earning

In the midsector of the curve—points 4, 5, and 6—organizations are in Earning, which means they are not in problem positions. Therefore, the focus is not so much on how to improve performance as it is on how to maintain current levels; not on how to move out of Entitlement or Fear but how to avoid moving out of Earning.

The three overall strategies, one for each point in the Earning sector of the Earning curve, are as follows:

Point 4:	Encourage risk taking.
Point 5:	Focus on sustaining excellence.
Point 6:	Encourage prudence.

And here, too, the strategies take slightly different forms depending on whether they are applied to organizations or to individuals.

For Organizations—What Executives Must Do

Point 4. *Encourage risk-taking.* This organization is productive and basically admirable, but it lacks the excitement of enjoying a higher level of risk. It is characterized more by prudence than by exhilaration. It's desirable to move this organization into 6 occasionally because a big win can excite the whole organization as well as those who specifically participated.

The basic message for leaders to communicate throughout the organization is "Don't try to get consensus so quickly; it creates too many compromises from the start of decision making. We need a leadership style that encourages thinking big, at least some of the time. Let's create a fund for innovative pilot projects. Let's go for a breakthrough!"

To stimulate risk taking, the organization must work toward creating small pockets of entrepreneurial activity, of "skunkworks." This may require hiring innovative leaders from outside, renting separate space, or allowing unique procedures and an autonomous budget. While suggestions for risky projects can come from the organization's executives, it's better to open the process to the organization as a whole.

Innovations and innovators should be widely publicized. Even if the project is only partially successful, it should be visible because it's a model of what the organization wants to increase. While most work will involve teams, rewards should go to individuals as well as to teams.

A good example to follow is 3M Corporation. Create the assumption that every year 15 to 20 percent of your products will be new and make rewards dependent on meeting that goal. The culture can say "We assume continuous improvement, but we reserve the largest rewards for breakthroughs."

The organization will train people in creative confrontation or healthy disagreement. Instead of focusing on amicable consensus, there needs to be agreement that divergent thinking provides creative potential. At 4, the organization's publicized goal should be "No more marching penguins."

Point 5. *Focus on sustaining excellence.* Without stress or crisis it's difficult to sustain maximum involvement and motivation. The leaders of the organization should be thinking "We have to be careful. We're in the most dangerous of conditions—we're doing great. It's very easy now to believe our own publicity and think we're perfect. Now's the time to really watch the competition. We're about to install assessment of all our operating units. Stay sharp!"

This organization will require change for its own sake. Goals must be continuously raised so the challenge is harder. Every so often, the structure is organized to create realignments, so that relationships change. Lateral transfers to different functions or kinds of responsibilities are a normal part of everyone's career.

Organizations at point 5 need to create an ongoing sense of competition with other companies, especially if they're large and powerful. Also, the organizations may profit from periodic reviews by impartial, knowledgeable outsiders.

This organization assumes continuous education. In addition to paying tuition, some people are sent, on the basis of competitive merit, to pursue degrees while on salary. This organization invests in people's creativity as well as knowledge as people earn sabbaticals. This organization requires a culture that presumes excellence.

Point 6. *Encourage prudence.* Often what we call innovation is not so much a gigantic breakthrough as an accumulation of small, incremental changes. In fact, as Michael Porter writes in the *Harvard Business Review,* "It often involves ideas that are not even 'new'—ideas that have been around, but never vigorously pursued."

Organizations that are at 6 do not give much attention to incremental modifications or progress. Applause is reserved for big breakthroughs. As a result, many smaller opportunities for improvement can be ignored. These organizations need to collect data within their own units, or within their competitors', demonstrating the cumulative effect of small gains, which can become very significant. There must be a factual demonstration that small gains are also a significant opportunity.

There's also the possibility that the pursuit of the big one threatens appropriate prudence. This organization needs procedures that impose some caution, procedures that slow the process slightly and require thoughtful consideration of alternatives, especially potential negative outcomes.

These procedures could involve, for example, reviews by special committees or a requirement that proposed decisions be formally defended before they are implemented. They could also involve training in formal techniques of problem solving, which could become a required style of making decisions. In this way the organization uses structure or rules of procedure to impose limits on impulsivity.

Organizations can be at 6 naturally, because they're entrepreneurial and they enjoy risk. They can also be at 6 (instead of 5) because management continuously exerts too much pressure for performance, with the result that people never quite gain any sense that they've earned security. That kind of pressure can be exerted vertically from the top down and also laterally by peers.

This organization needs to lighten up. Pressures that are not being created out of the reality of competition or other work conditions should be lessened, including not making fine distinctions between performers. Limit the number of performance categories to a few; then the great majority of employees will be evaluated as "very good," and very few will be judged as "outstanding" or "unsatisfactory."

The criteria of performance must be high, but there should be no limit on how many people are permitted to succeed. Don't use one-on-one competition or ranking with this population because then every winner makes other people losers. While employees may be able to earn bonuses, no part of their salary should be at risk. As almost everyone performs very well, there should be few distinctions between them in the rewards they can and do earn.

For Individuals—What Managers Must Do

Point 4. *Encourage risk taking.* For individuals who seem to be at point 4, continually encourage them to stretch. They should be hearing this message from their managers: "I know it's a nice feeling to be a member of the team, but every time you have a big idea and the others don't cheer right away, you seem to back off. Remember, breakthrough ideas mean you're either coming out of left field or you're way ahead of the pack. Give the others time to catch up with you. Don't give up so easily."

Point 5. *Focus on sustaining excellence.* Position 5 is the ideal state. People who've reached 5 tend to stay there, as being a 5 comes to be a critical part of their self-esteem. Managers can nourish and maintain this state by communicating this basic message: "You are terrific and I want you to know how much we appreciate your contributions. You are an outstanding performer in an excellent team. Do you have any ideas that I haven't heard about for improving your own or your group's performance even more?"

Point 6. *Encourage prudence.* Managers might say "I really admire your innovativeness. You're ready to take on challenges that would scare most people. But sometimes I think your follow-through isn't as good as it could be. A lot of improvements come from making the details better. Think about finding a partner who likes to do that kind of work."

Make Yourself the Model

When you are trying to optimize performance, your basic strategy is to encourage 4's to take bigger risks and to ease 6's toward greater prudence. One way is to be a model of what you want to see. To encourage others toward greater risk taking, you could publicly show your willingness to take on longer projects or initiate more substantial change than usual. To demonstrate prudence, you could made decisions based largely on precedent, and make sure people know that's your basis. Depending on the need, you can pay attention to or ignore the guidelines of custom; you can challenge or support the cultural assumptions.

In a more directive strategy, managers can require that subordinates analyze assumptions and determine whether they're still appropriate. They can require changes in the styles of how decisions are made, pushing their people toward either more risk or a bit more caution. They can designate individuals who use the preferred style as a formal leader.

The more important issue is for management not to behave in ways that demotivate this group. This population consists of people who are sufficiently excellent that management must be careful not to burden them with work that isn't important. Because they're likely to be experts, which is an advantage for management, managers may tend to keep these people doing the same work for longer than is optimal for the employee. Management must create opportunities for new responsibilities, risk, and learning.

With these excellent performers, don't tell; instead, consult, collaborate, and participate. Assume excellence and verbalize that assumption.

Creating the Conditions of Earning

To get commitment and high performance, organizations need to create the conditions that will give people opportunities to be winners. Companies at points 4, 5, and 6 need most of all to nurture the creative energy that is already buzzing throughout the place. Imagine all employees were volunteers. What would motivate them to come to work?

"What I'm doing is significant. It makes a difference. *I* make a difference."

"What I'm doing is important and it has an impact on something I care about."

"I really care about this stuff and I'm one of the people who's making it happen."

"I'm really challenged. I keep on growing and the leash is long."

"My ideas are respected. I have a lot of say in what gets done and how it's done."

"It's fun! It's a great group of people and we're in it together. We're winning!"

Where people have those kinds of attitudes toward their work, you have an environment of Earning.

Do those statements sound familiar? Think back to the section in Chapter 4 that described the three conditions that motivate people, that give them a sense of job enrichment:

1. Challenge
2. Empowerment
3. Significance

Remember that we discovered these are the same conditions that nurture productivity and innovation? Thus, we can say that the task of maintaining a climate where Earning can thrive is the task of converting those three psychological needs into management actions.

Challenge

Challenge is the opportunity to learn or master something new. It inevitably means risk, since people who try something new can never be certain they'll succeed. Risk is a vital part of the experience of challenge and is the core of the sense of having fun at work. When people say they want challenge, they're saying they want to learn, to do different work, and to push to the edge of their comfort zone.

I often ask people "What have you ever done that gave you a special sense of accomplishment?" In answer, they almost never refer to something that got them a reward of some kind. Instead, they remember the times when they stood up to risk and succeeded. They say things like:

> "I was required to get technical training, which I would never have done, and when I was finished I wrote a paper and it got published."
> "I created a training program against lots of opposition and it was terrific."
> "I went into work where there were no other women."
> "I made the presentation of our project, and it was to people who were all senior to me."

"I had to negotiate some tricky clauses with the union and I did it and we all felt like we'd won."
"I was asked to do a special assignment that involved automating our compensation system and I hadn't had any computer experience up to then."

As people meet this kind of challenge, they learn a lot:

"It was an exciting time."
"I learned to really delegate."
"I found people loved being part of the team."
"I found everybody has more ability than they ever knew, and that includes me."

Require the Stretch

Organizations can always create opportunities for people to be challenged. The key is to raise your expectations. High expectations are terrific motivators. When little is expected, little is given. In organizations with a psychology of Earning, the basic assumption is that everyone is capable of achieving and succeeding. The culture of the organization will take that for granted. People generally perform at the level they are expected to perform.

Tolerate Mistakes

Another thing we must do, if we genuinely want to stimulate challenge, is learn to tolerate mistakes. A culture of Earning must include the sense that it's okay to make some mistakes because that will happen with innovation and learning, especially when the challenge is complex. Although no organization can tell employees to simply plow ahead and not to worry about making errors, there has to be an attitude that reasonable and occasional mistakes are opportunities to learn something.

In August 1990, Pacific Bell's top leadership held a day-long meeting to introduce to middle managers a new organizational structure that PacBell believes will permit greater focus on customers and markets. Following the presentation, the team answered questions from the audience.

QUESTION FROM AN EMPLOYEE: Often, people learn best by failing. Are you willing to tolerate failure? Do you think it is required?

BOB LEE *(executive vice-president, statewide markets):* Clearly we're moving into an environment where we have to accept risk. I have a pen that says "Eight out of ten is better than three out of three." In the past, we've been a business that aimed for—and got—three out of three, and it took us a long time to do that. We have to become the kind of company that shoots for—and gets—eight out of ten.

PHIL QUIGLEY *(president and CEO):* One of my mentors was the man who invented the Mickey Mouse telephone—he literally broke the telephone barrier with respect to product. I asked him once when we were flying together what the difference was between the corporate type and the entrepreneurial type. He said the corporate type has all the resources and all the time to make a decision—and they make those decisions right 98 percent of the time. The entrepreneurial type probably makes the right decision six out of ten times—but they're the decisions that really make an impact.

Promote Self-Challenging

While organizations, in the form of managers, can give people developmental or challenge experiences, it's very important that individuals themselves realize there are always opportunities for learning, if they'll look for them. People who work in large organizations especially are prone to wait for the organization to create the experience. Instead, people ought to be held responsible for finding and initiating these opportunities for themselves, because that can result in a greater sense of personal power and confidence than stepping up to an assignment they did nothing to generate.

In that kind of environment, continuously moving into what's new or meeting a challenge will be taken for granted, because that's the usual thing people do. Change will be at the core of ordinary routine. People will look for chances to contribute to the mainstream and improve the business where it counts.

If the circumstances are really good, there'll be ways for everyone to compete and win, and so competitive hostility will be directed outward, to the institution's competition. That's exactly what's happening in Industrial Computer Source, the company we visited in the beginning of Chapter 4.

Empowerment

Empowerment means sharing power, increasing autonomy, throughout the organization. It means giving everyone—instead of just people with certain positions or certain job titles—the legitimate right to make judgments, form conclusions, reach decisions, and then act. The point is not to spread power around willy-nilly but to pinpoint it, to move the decision as close as possible to the point where action can be taken: on the production line, on the shop floor, in the back office, in the functional departments.

Respect the Many Forms of Achievement

The process of empowerment is based on the recognition that good ideas can come from anywhere, that achievement takes many forms and all of them deserve respect. Coping with change is the major impetus for listening to anyone, at any grade, who has something to offer. That's why empowerment is a required management style when things are different or unpredictable. Familiarity with or a mastery of what happened before isn't always the best guide for what should be done now, when there's a lot of change. When the risks are high and so are the unknowns, it's necessary to pull together as a team. When you have to master the unknown, you're more prone to listen to whoever learns the fastest or knows the most, wherever they are on the ladder.

I learned that in an unexpected way with two of my children. When they were adolescents, aged fifteen and sixteen, our family set out on a year-long trip wandering around Central and South America. We, their parents, had not anticipated how irrelevant our professional skills would be. What we did at home that gave us formal power—being professors of nuclear physics and psychology—were not exactly critical skills when we were trying to buy fruit and vegetables from Native Americans in their outdoor market.

It turned out that the sixteen-year-old was the world's second best navigator, the first being Magellan. Unflappable, she'd sit in the copilot's seat and direct the driver through urban sprawl or mountain crags. She also turned out to be really talented in language, and within two months she could manage in Spanish. The fifteen-year-old was a good car mechanic when we started out. Six months into the trip, he'd become an excellent mechanic. He was also a hotshot at bargaining, an integral part of life in that culture.

Under ordinary circumstances, American adolescents are tolerated by their parents who are praying they won't get into trouble and waiting for them to grow up. In the usual conditions, our teenagers don't have skills or knowledge that allow them to earn the respect of adults as peers. On that trip, the two kids had skills we needed; they were better in some necessary things than their parents. As they did those things, they earned our respect. While they were always our children, they also became our peers much of the time.

Diminish the Hierarchy

In an empowering organization there's a generalized assumption that everybody is competent, if not yet, then after they've had a chance to learn. People in these organizations have developed the belief that what they accomplish is at least as important as their formal status or rank in the hierarchy. They believe that real contributions earn them the right to influence others. In other words, empowering organizations will give different kinds of people opportunities to lead. Thus, empowering organizations will have several kinds of leadership derived from different kinds of power.

Another thing we must do to create the conditions where Earning can flourish is rid ourselves of the caste system mentality that goes with a rigid hierarchy. We must begin to see workers at all levels as assets, not problems to be managed by a few decision makers at the top.

A caste system is dispiriting and demotivating because no matter how well you work or how much you know, until you get on the higher rungs of the ladder you can't get recognized as a significant player. Of course, that leads to a lack of involvement and, in the long run, a disinterest in working toward common goals for the good of the organization.

Shaking off this caste way of thinking will not be easy. U.S. industry has operated in a hierarchical mode for many years, starting with the "efficient" operations of auto makers in the early twentieth century, where a few at the top made decisions for the many on the assembly lines and those at the bottom were expected to do what they were told. But now, in the reality of worldwide competition, American institutions are painfully learning the cost of this legacy of not involving employees at all levels in continual problem solving. A psychologically hierarchical organization loses input from subordinates at all levels, including professionals and management.

New Management Attitudes

Empowered people are supposed to think and evaluate; input is expected from everyone. In a practical sense, that means managers do a lot of listening. Those higher up in the hierarchy make sure they hear those who are lower down.

If people are to be empowered, management has to believe that the person who does the work knows more about it than anyone else and is therefore the best one to improve how it is done. Deep down, many managers still believe they have more experience than workers. They may be willing to listen, but they are rarely willing to let lower-level people—the ones actually doing the work—make the decisions.

We need to set up what Robert Waterman calls "directed autonomy." This idea simply means there are boundaries as well as freedoms: People have to know what their boundaries are. They need to know when they can act on their own and when they should consult with their boss. The boss has to establish the boundaries and decide when to require consultation and when to get out of the way. Managers create the space within which people can be autonomous, and outside of which there are limits to their freedom to act. In a good organization, one where people are required to be responsible for themselves, the individual and the organization will collaborate in ways that make the space larger and larger. It's another way to think about what empowerment involves.

It may require a mind-set shift. Mangers have to give up attitudes of superiority. They have to stop thinking "I have to tell them what to do and how to do it." They have to give up the idea that "If I'm not watching and judging, they'll do a lousy job." Giving up this authoritarian view has a direct payback: the end of adversarial relations.

New Employee Attitudes

Jack Welch, the dynamic CEO of General Electric, describes the ideal manager–employee relationship:

> Ultimately, we're talking about redefining the relationship between the boss and the subordinate. I want to get to a point where people challenge their bosses every day: "Why do you require me to do these wasteful things? Why don't you let me do the things you shouldn't be doing so you can move on and create? That's the job of a leader—to create, not to control. Trust me to do my job, and don't make me waste all my time trying to deal with you on the control issue."
>
> [People] will develop the personal courage to speak out. The norm will become the person who says, "Dammit, we're not doing it. Let's get on with doing it." . . . This process will create more fulfilling and rewarding jobs. The quality of work life will improve dramatically.

New Leader Attitudes

It's fashionable to talk about empowerment right now, and some of what is said is too sweet. Empowering organizations are not led by Ms. or Mr. Pollyanna. I've always found that the leaders in those organizations became leaders because they're among the smartest of a group of really smart people. And they're very comfortable being judgmental. They have earned their position of authority and are very outspoken. But they don't need to embellish their power, so they use the word *participatory* a lot. They say their job is to set a strategic direction and get people to buy into it, to give others money and authority, and then to leave them alone to do the work. In discussions they listen a lot as they also prod and challenge.

Reuben Mark, CEO of Colgate-Palmolive, is one such leader. He says "The more [power] you have, the less you should use. You consolidate and build power by empowering others. I don't like to talk about power. I prefer to think of it as responsibility and authority."

Ralph Stayer, CEO of Johnsonville Foods, said "Real power is getting people committed. Real power comes from giving it up to others who are in a better position to do things than you are." And he puts his words into action. Since 1985 people from Johnsonville's shop floor have written the manufacturing budget; they volunteer for the task. Another group of volunteers designs the manufacturing line. If the workers want new equipment, they work up the cash flow analysis.

Stayer's approach is to establish a climate in which goals are set as far down in the company as possible; top managers then spend their time choosing which goals should have first claim on the company's capital. In 1988, for instance, the sales department set a goal of increasing sales volume by 40 percent, and the manufacturing group backed them up by setting their own goal of providing the additional output while holding cost increases to 20 percent.

Since 1983, Johnsonville has doubled its return on assets, and sales have increased more than 15 percent a year—twice as fast as the payroll.

Significance

Most of us need to feel that our work matters: "It matters that I do it and it's important enough that it better be done well.

I have to take my work seriously because there are important consequences if it's done well or badly. What I do now will have an impact on me and this organization (or occupation) in the future. I'm not wasting my time going through the motions. This is important and I take it seriously."

In contrast, people don't feel their work is significant if the following is true:

- It's not obviously connected to what that organization's business is.
- It doesn't result in something that can be measured in terms of outcome or impact.
- It's work that fulfills bureaucratic requirements and involves shuffling papers and/or going to endless meetings.

Researchers Lorsch and Takagi found that people remained exceptionally committed to their work when their job involved responsibilities that contributed to the company. When their performance had an impact on the organization's results, they felt significant. When their efforts led to success for the organization, they felt like winners. In short, they had the sense that they counted and they had an impact on the present and the future of the organization. And the organization was important to them, so it was important that they do their work well.

Organizations have tried to help people feel their work is significant by showing them how it ultimately contributes to the company. Of course, that helps, but it's not the most effective thing they can do. More important, I think, is to do the work of figuring out how each person can contribute to what the business really does.

All employees with their supervisors should think through these questions:

- What is my function?
- What do I contribute?
- How do I make a difference?

Then management should allow people to increase those significant aspects of their job and reduce or eliminate as much as possible of the rest.

It's a good idea for supervisors and managers to routinely ask people if they think their work contributes and ask how they think they might contribute more. It's conceivable that people have very different opinions about what is significant.

One of the best things companies can do for people who are not in the mainstream of the business is to assign them to temporary committees or task forces that are engaged in significant projects. I once asked a person in a major computer manufacturing company what her job was. She was embarrassed. In a company known for state-of-the-art product development, her job was to keep the organizational chart current. As people changed their job, she changed the chart in the mainframe computer. The work, we might argue, was necessary, but it wasn't significant. She needed an opportunity to feel that she made a real difference.

If I were her manager I'd ask her to look around and find activities, programs, committees, and task forces that she'd like to do as part of her job. If she didn't find any, I'd made a few suggestions. (In theory I guess we might also try to find someone who thought keeping the chart current was an important thing to do.)

In an article about how Korea won the microwave war, Ira Magaziner and Mark Patinkin describe a worker named Hwang. Her job is to attach the serial numbers and name-brand labels to Samsung microwave ovens. She attaches about 1,200 labels a day. Six days a week, hour after hour, she does the same simple thing. Even after the inspector has double-checked her work, she herself checks it one more time.

She says her job is a challenge to her personal discipline, thus to her integrity. "I put my spirit, my soul, in this product." If you do it perfectly every time, she says, you are teaching yourself excellence. And Hwang remembers it wasn't so long ago that Korea was poor. It's not poor anymore. Hwang believes that she is contributing to something very important—to Korea itself. On many levels, this mundane task is significant to her.

Doing work that is significant also can mean finding opportunity for personal expression in a job. We want to feel that what we do is enduring. That purpose provides the motive toward excellence. It's not about money. It's about our psychological need to feel that our work expands the purpose and meaning of our life; money is just a way of keeping score.

Not long ago, billionaire Warren Buffett visited the Nebraska Furniture Mart that his company, Berkshire Hathaway, company, had acquired. He spend the day with Mrs. Rose Blumkin, who established the store fifty years ago with $500. Today the store is the largest of its kind and Mrs. Blumkin is ninety-four years old. She's at work seven days a week. She gets around in an electric golf cart and says she's having a ball.

Neither Mr. Buffett nor Mrs. Blumkin needs money. Buffett says "Money is a by-product of something I like to do very much. Every day, when I get to the office, so to speak, I do a little tap dance."

9

The New Paradigm

Since the mid-1970s, we have tumbled from our perch of economic dominance. Although it hurts, the fall has the potential of galvanizing us to new ways of thinking and working that will serve us far better in the 1990s.

The 1980s began with the deepest postwar recession we ever had. We had double-digit inflation and interest rates. OPEC tried to strangle the economy. Many manufacturers struggled to survive and many didn't. Our budget deficit and our trade deficit were alarming. Competition increased on all sides at a frightening rate, and old-line companies, long dominant in their industry, found themselves uncompetitive.

Yet Americans seem to be driven by crisis. During the 1980s, as things got worse, many things got better. Many U.S. manufacturers got lean and aggressive. Many reorganized. Some of the changes were wrenching: firings, voluntary early retirements, leveraged buyouts, mergers, and acquisitions.

The result is that we've become competitive in many sectors of industry. Many who found themselves losing in international competition have learned to create quality and value. Our economy created an incredible number of new jobs. Though huge, our deficits are now a smaller percentage of our economy than they were.

Despite all the gloom, our economy is stronger than pessimists contend and our standard of living remains the highest in the world. Using purchasing power parities (a measure of what the same amount of money would buy in another country), the Bureau of Labor Statistics has calculated that in 1988

West Germany's purchase value was 72 percent of U.S. levels and Japan's was 81 percent.

On the other hand, we still have large sectors of the economy within which Entitlement flourishes. And, when I look at survivors within those organizations that downsized, reorganized, merged, and fired, I fear we are again in danger of decline. During downsizing or after the merger or buyout, there's a lot of fear. Because the downsizing is a necessary response to a loss of market share or a decrease in tax revenues, people usually respond with increased efforts to make things better. As long as the anxiety is not paralyzingly high, productivity rises.

But when the crisis is over, so is the sense of alarm.

In organizations where Entitlement prevailed, what I see after the crisis seems to pass is the reinstatement of Entitlement. When the worst seems over, a reality of no risk is recreated. This situation, I believe, is what happened at Kodak.

The Kodak Experience

In 1983, Colby Chandler became chairman and chief executive officer of the century-old company that one analyst has called a "bureaucratic behemoth." Almost immediately, the company laid off thousands of workers, for the first time in corporate history. I was there, and it was surrealistic. People continued to go to meetings and chat, and no one said anything about the layoffs.

The next year, profits were up by 63 percent, and then started to slip; a second restructuring was announced. Through 1985 and part of 1986, the company had six straight quarters of losses. Another restructuring took place: 10,000 more people were laid off and a cost-cutting program was set up. Profits more than tripled the following year, and set a record in 1988, when net profit increased 60 percent over 1985, and net earnings were up by 322 percent. Then, in 1989, profits fell by 23 percent in the first quarter, and the company announced cost-cutting plans that included more layoffs. All in all, the company went through four separate restructurings in seven years, eliminating some 25,000 employees, including managers. In that time, long-term debt increased from less than 5 percent of total capital to more than 46 percent.

What was happening? There was increased competition, a periodic rise in the value of the dollar, and high expenses associated with the 1988 acquisition of Sterling Drug Company. But it is also plausible that Kodak, which enjoyed unequalled Entitlement for more than a century, keeps reverting back to it as soon as the pressure of a crisis passes. One stock analyst observing the period of ups and downs commented in mid-1989 that "It seems like they wipe their brow and say, 'Whew, we're glad that's over,' and then they turn around and have to do it all over again."

A related factor, of course, is the leadership of Kodak. Chandler, who at first seemed determined to breathe life into the "behemoth," made changes that most observers consider too slow and too gentle. In mid-1989, after those seven years of reorganizations, analysts still characterized Kodak as a benevolent corporate father and Chandler as a paternalistic caretaker. "Their idea of dramatic cost-cutting and dramatic restructuring isn't that dramatic. They still have a mentality that is somewhat paternalistic."

And where are they now? In June 1989, the "tough-talking" Kay Whitmore took over as chairman and CEO. Late that year, he put in place yet another restructuring, cutting 4,500 workers and linking managers' compensation directly to corporate profits. Is it working? The jury's still out, but one analyst has commented "This company has tried perennially to cost cut. It has become evident that this time they are succeeding."

New Leadership Style for a New Era

Shaking out of Entitlement is a profound change, and it must be accompanied by changes in management style. Increasingly, today's strategies for creating change reflect the paradigm shift toward empowerment. Today's progressive leaders need to know how to get people to work as collaborative teams, and that is a very different skill from what managers were expected to possess fifteen years ago.

Management's task, therefore, is increasingly one of setting direction and then motivating and harnessing the collective and creative energies of everyone involved. Ralph Stayer, CEO of Johnsonville Foods, describes this change in terms of power, which of course is exactly what it is:

> Before, I didn't have power because I had people wandering around not giving a damn. Real power is getting people committed. Real power comes from giving it up to others who are in a better position to do things than you are. Control is an illusion. The only control you can possibly have comes when people are controlling themselves.

The new style of managing is based on the idea that other people may know more about something than you do, even though your status is higher. At IBM, for example, when an engineer gets stuck on a problem it may be entered into the computer and ideas may be received from 70,000 people. Simultaneously, the entire organization can work on a problem.

Solving the problems, moving toward the goals, is increasingly the task of teams of workers who come together in shifting combinations. As William Taylor wrote, "Corporate cultures have to move toward a philosophy of shared problems and challenges—task forces that arise from the mist, attack a problem, and then go away."

In the new paradigm, managers and supervisors who are accustomed to being in control are now being asked to give that control over to the people they manage. Many find this task difficult. It is common to find a lot of confusion and high levels of anxiety among supervisors and managers in organizations shifting from the old paradigm to the new. Some will not be able to make the transition and will have to be replaced. But even those who successfully change may continue to experience more uncertainty about their role than is optimal.

Therefore, supervisors and managers need a considerable period of strong support. That support must come first from the executive level. The organization's leadership must provide statements about style and values, must create and fund strong management development programs, and must create opportunities for supervisors and managers to meet and discuss issues relevant to them. It's also helpful if support, in the form of nonadversarial behavior, comes from the employees as well. This tends to happen naturally when employees share the values and are given opportunities to learn about and offer input for changes.

The New Employment Contract

The old employment contract, founded in the psychology of Entitlement, promised almost absolute job security. The new contract, founded on Earning, promises job security of a different sort. The criteria for success and for belonging will rest on achievement.

The new contract says "If you are productive and add value, if you keep on learning and your skills are current, you'll be okay. In fact, our half of the bargain is to keep creating opportunities for you to achieve. Your half of the bargain is to keep on achieving."

For the employees' part, people feel more secure when the organization's basic attitude is that people who work there are competent, honest, and intelligent. That implies the organization will not be tricky in how it deals with people. And those feelings of security are increased when the organization makes commitments to its employees as part of its formal corporate values, like IBM's "Respect for the Individual" (see sidebar).

IBM's Guiding Principles: Respect for the Individual

Our basic belief is respect for the individual, for each person's rights and dignity. It follows from this principle that IBM should:

a.   Help employees develop their potential and make the best use of their abilities.

b. Pay and promote on merit.
c. Maintain two-way communications between manager and employee, with opportunity for a fair hearing and equitable settlement of disagreements.

Another aspect of security is knowing that the company will be straight with you. People feel more secure when they know the truth about where they stand and how their organization is doing. Trust that comes from long-term honest communication is an important factor in the psychology of Earning. Organizations do better when they don't clobber people, but they also don't evade the hard issues.

Another part of the new contract is a mutual understanding that people's performance on the job—and nothing else—determines their success or failure. Evaluation procedures must protect people from prejudiced and idiosyncratic behavior on the part of superiors. Furthermore, this performance/rewards balance must be genuine. Unless there is a direct relationship between levels of performance directed to specific outcomes and what happens to people, all you have is empty talk.

We know that people respond to what they're held accountable for. If companies tell employees to "pay attention to your customer" but actually measure the amount of product that is shipped out the door, then good customer service doesn't really count.

To get employees to pay attention to the customer, you must hold them specifically accountable for customer service. The evaluation of their performance has to be tied directly to the goal of satisfying the customer. If they add to customer satisfaction, they should be rewarded. If they don't increase customer satisfaction, some penalty must occur. Slogans by themselves are irrelevant.

It is increasingly clear that employees are capable of doing excellent work and will do it when excellence is expected and when they understand why excellence is important. The new contract, in summary, defines the new kind of organization we need to be working toward. In the new paradigm:

- People at all levels are given the opportunity to show what they can do. There are lots of leaders.
- Most work is done in small teams of peers, led by people who are knowledgeable in the particular area of concern.
- People are given continuous challenges, along with support.
- Managers are coaches, not dictators.
- Ability and contribution count more than status.
- Rewards reflect real contribution.
- Accountability is enthusiastically embraced, as people see a direct payoff.

The Dynamics of Change

A reversal of values is a huge change. Those who are trying to make it happen need to have a clear vision of what they want to accomplish; they need to measure progress and broadcast those results to everyone, and they must have patience.

They need patience because major change takes a long time. Jack Bowsher found it took smaller organizations five years to implement a fundamental change in just their educational system, and large organizations take eight to ten. Unless a crisis threatens, making the need for changes inescapably obvious, a change to Earning, to empowerment, and to accountability will take at least that long.

It's easy to lose sight of the real problem. When organizations don't keep that in the center of their vision, their solutions go not to the core where the real issue is but instead to the periphery. Then attention is directed to creating a mission statement or teaching team building. While those peripheral solutions may be important and constructive, addressing them is not sufficiently motivating. Only when there's a sense of danger do you get real energy and long-term commitment to deal with the pain and anxiety of change.

Therefore, to get fundamental change on an organization-wide basis, find either (1) a part of the organization that is in real trouble—danger looms if it doesn't change, so there is a real reason for the change—or (2) a part of the organization that has had a real problem, made changes, and thus had the experience of converting the problem into an opportunity.

Many well-intentioned change programs fail because there is a lack of understanding of how the change process works. Organizations assume that the place to start is with the individual: Get individuals to change and automatically the organization changes too. This belief is exactly backward. Behavior of employees, as individuals, is powerfully affected by their role in the organization. Therefore, the most direct route to change is to give people a new role.

That's what my recommendations concerning increasing or decreasing people's sense of risk are intended to do. I'm not suggesting that you try and talk people into changing how they behave (although I do recommend explaining what you are doing and why). Rather, I'm describing ways in which organizations can alter the conditions of work. I'm describing ways companies can create change in the conditions of people's experience. Then, because there are negative or positive consequences to what people do, behavior changes. And then, attitudes will change too.

Personally, I don't believe people change in response to concepts or abstractions. They change because they need to, because they feel there's a real danger if they don't change. Leaders can encourage and foster change, but in the end it rests on the shoulders of the employees who will be affected.

The New Paradigm Taking Shape at Ford

It's hard to imagine a company more American than Ford Motor Company. For years, Ford products have symbolized American enterprise. Ford was so solid that it forgot about the customer. When the economic picture began to change in the 1970s, no one in Detroit was paying attention.

Lee Miskowski is a vice-president and general manager of the Parts and Service Division. In an eloquent and dramatic speech delivered in 1987, he describes the trouble that began in the late 1970s—economic recession, oil embargoes, and frightening competition from Japan—that "changed forever the environment in which we do business."

The effect on Ford was catastrophic: three straight years of billion-dollar losses. Miskowski says "We lost more money in those three years than we made in the first eighty years of our corporate history." At first there was nothing but a kind of corporate disbelief. Another Ford executive describes the reaction:

> The first year the loss was a total surprise. We had no idea things were that bad. No one imagined we'd do it a second time. The third year we were absolutely amazed. There was a lot of denial, but we got the message: Something was terribly, fundamentally wrong.

Ford demonstrated the truth we have learned: If things are bad enough, change is possible, even in the most entrenched bureaucracies. Miskowski explains:

> For the first time, I think, we came down from our ivory towers. We were literally shocked into understanding that we had become comfortable with some inefficient, outdated ways of thinking and working that simply had to be replaced.

Both Ford executives I talked with agreed that the most important element in turning things around was the company's top leadership. "Good leadership at the top was critical in saving us. There was a clear message: We had to change or we'd be out of business. Then there was the meeting with the executives and Mr. Ford made his speech." Lee Miskowski picks up the story:

> Every four or five years we have a three-day meeting of our top 500 managers from around the world. . . . [At the meeting] in November 1984, . . . everybody really waited to hear from Henry Ford II. And when he got up to speak, he didn't talk about product, or economics, or profits, or any of the other things he could have chosen. Instead, Mr. Ford devoted his entire speech to one thing: our corporate culture. How are we going to live our corporate lives, and what values do we want to live by?

That speech galvanized the company. It inspired the artic-
ulation of the values statement that is now known as MVGP—
Mission, Values, and Guiding Principles (see sidebar). It is not
an empty document. It is, as Miskowski says, "our bill of rights
and responsibilities," and it is the foundation of an amazing
success story.

New Values in Operation

Miskowski relates some of the highlights of how they went
about putting the guiding principles into action.

Quality

That word is so pervasive in everything we do at Ford
that we practically eat it for breakfast. And we mean
quality in the broadest sense: every job, hourly and
salaried, related to some aspect of quality. . . . It's
amazing: When the quality is right (or at least improving) everything else seems to fall into place.

Customer Focus

We're now running the business on the simple premise that we're here to satisfy our customers. And that
. . . is the single most significant event culturally that
has occurred in our history. We finally have gone
from a mentality that said, "We are smarter than the
customer," to one that essentially is willing to admit
that, in fact, we are not. And we now understand that
it is the customer's interests—as complex as those interests may be—that we must listen and react to.

Of course, quality and customer focus are related, and
Ford has recognized this link with its top-quality committee, a
group that is charged with examining fundamentals. The
group is divided into three subgroups, each one focused on one
part of the quality strategy. The first subgroup defines quality
from the customer's point of view, and feeds that to the second
group, which is developing an internal system that allows the

FORD

Mission

Ford Motor Company is a worldwide leader in automotive and auto-related products and services as well as in newer industries such as aerospace, communications, and financial services. Our mission is to improve continually our products and services to meet our customers' needs, allowing us to prosper as a business and to provide a reasonable return for our stockholders, the owners of our business.

Values

How we accomplish our mission is as important as the mission itself. Fundamental to success for the Company are these basic values:

People—Our people are the source of our strength. They provide our corporate intelligence and determine our reputation and vitality. Involvement and teamwork are our core human values.

Products—Our products are the end result of our efforts, and they should be the best in serving customers worldwide. As our products are viewed, so are we viewed.

Profits—Profits are the ultimate measure of how efficiently we provide customers with the best products for their needs. Profits are required to survive and grow.

Guiding Principles

Quality comes first—To achieve customer satisfaction, the quality of our products and services must be our number one priority.

Customers are the focus of everything we do—Our work must be done with our customers in mind, providing better products and services than our competition.

Continuous improvement is essential to our success—We must strive for excellence in everything we do: in our products, in their safety and value—and in our services, our human relations, our competitiveness, and our profitability.

Employee involvement is our way of life—We are a team. We must treat each other with trust and respect.

Dealers and suppliers are our partners—The Company must maintain mutually beneficial relationships with dealers, suppliers, and our other business associates.

Integrity is never compromised—The conduct of our Company worldwide must be pursued in a manner that is socially responsible and commands respect for its integrity and for its positive contributions to society. Our doors are open to men and women alike without discrimination and without regard to ethnic origin or personal beliefs.

company to meet those customer expectations. The third group facilitates the changes in the corporate culture that are necessary for success in the quality focus.

Employee Involvement

We have learned some interesting things in the last few years. Employees have great ideas. Our new products have incorporated hundreds of ideas from the assembly worker on up. And of course this breeds pride and a sense of belonging.

It also breeds success. Ford has a plant in Batavia, Ohio, that manufactures a particular component also produced by a Mazda plant in Japan and sold to Ford. Ford leaders were thinking about closing down the Batavia plant because the Mazda parts were better and cheaper. Then, six months after the team concept started in 1985, the workers at Batavia saved their own jobs: Through employee involvement teams, they figured out how to make the part more cheaply than Mazda and of better quality.

As part of the employee involvement principle, Ford instituted Team Taurus; it is a fine example of a cross-skill team. Miskowski describes how it works:

Teamwork

The former way of cycling the development of a product from organization to organization (design concepts, advanced engineering, product development, etc.) and then finally hand it over to the assembly system and say "You build it" and to sales operations and say "You sell it" was thrown out in favor of a teamwork process. Now elements of every major component are involved in the entire process right from the beginning. The advantages are so obvious that one wonders what took us so long to come to this conclusion.

According to Miskowski, support for the team concept originated with then CEO Donald Petersen. In his speech, he incorporated this story from *AdWeek* magazine:

Petersen believes so strongly in the Team Ford concept that when *Motor Trend* magazine wanted to name him Man of the Year, he flatly refused the honor. Instead he put together a symbolic team with a member representing each department, from design to the production line, to accept the award. And, when the same magazine picked Taurus car of the year, award certificates were printed up for everyone who worked on the assembly line.

New Leadership

There appears to be universal agreement that the new leadership at Ford, embodied in CEO Don Petersen and President (now CEO) Harold ("Red") Poling, is truly different. Petersen recalls the old days at Ford, infamous for political infighting, personality clashes, bloody battles for power: "Those days built into me a strong desire to see things work differently."

And things indeed changed. Jack Telnack, chief of design, tells about the time Petersen looked over his shoulder at some preliminary designs and asked Telnack if he himself would drive a car like that. Telnack decided to be candid: "Absolutely not. I wouldn't want that car parked in my driveway." So Petersen told him to get busy and design something he would be proud of, and the result was the highly successful Taurus.

The Ford Philosophy Today

The question now is, Will this new culture sustain us now that we are experiencing hard times again? Overall, the mood at Ford seems to be "These are very tough days. But we've shown we can be winners. Let's weather it. Let's be very competitive."

The industry is cyclical and competition for customers, especially with the Japanese manufacturing presence in the United States, is unending. Despite the fact that Ford has achieved great gains in productivity, quality, and technology, in fact, Ford posted a loss of $884.4 million in the first quarter of 1991 and is not expected to show a profit for the year. We cannot know with certainty what its future will be like. It is not the only automaker in trouble. The Big Three U.S. auto manufacturers may have a combined loss of $3 billion in the first quarter of 1991. Sales are also down significantly for Toyota, Nissan, Honda, Subaru, Isuzu, and Mazda.

The transformation of Ford from Entitlement to Earning was a necessity in terms of achieving success in today's competitive marketplace. It enabled the company to triumph over competitors, especially with the Taurus, the most successful American car of the 1980s.

But transforming an organization's culture and structure does not insulate a company or an industry from hard realities that it does not control: The U.S. economy is in recession. Unemployment is rising and could reach 7 percent by the end of the year.

The banking system is in grave trouble, and so are major corporations. Eastern Air Lines and Federated Department Stores, for example, are in Chapter 11 bankruptcy proceedings.

The economic news is gloomy. Thus, consumers are not spending. They are not buying cars or much else. Consumer spending is in one of the sharpest slowdowns on record and is a primary cause of the recession. The downturn has impacted virtually all regions of the country as well as most industries.

In this climate, about 20 percent of the banks have become "somewhat less willing" to make consumer loans. Car dealers report they are selling cars, but the deals fall through because they can't get financing. And consumers, who are laden with debt, are increasingly reluctant to borrow and buy as the Recession continues.

In 1990, over one million individuals filed for bankruptcy, and 1.2 million bankruptcies are predicted for 1991. Real incomes are declining. Cutbacks are continuing. Even people whose incomes place them in the top 20 percent no longer feel safe.

Those people are worrying about keeping their middle management jobs and about paying their mortgages and the costs of college. The 1980s psychology of affluence appears to have been replaced, at least for now, by caution.

Thus, consumers are retrenching. No matter how vital your organization or how excellent your customer service or how exciting your product, as long as customers are worried and cautious, sales will fall.

But organizations, including Ford, which were in Earning, are far better positioned than those that never got there to re-create success when the economy, and thus consumer attitudes, improves.

Having survived the years of catastrophic crisis, Ford has learned some things:

- Because of the crisis, it was able to focus on quality and to get an excellent product.
- Relationships between people changed. You could see it at meetings.
- The winners, the people who keep getting promoted now, are the ones who espouse and support the new culture.
- Ford evolved a methodology based on consensus.
- There are teams of cross-functional people working together.

- The new hero transcends the narrow experience of the traditional kind of organization employees.
- People leave their old turf in which they've become mired and they move into new territory.
- Ford hires 5's, people who are driven not only by external rewards but also by internal passion.

One Ford executive comments on the depth of the changes: "The idea that employees should be empowered, that we need teamwork, and that management should be participative and involved was very new for us. There's still some tendency to go back to the old ways, but we're a much more democratic organization than we used to be."

We should also note the very positive changes in relationships between management and union. In the early 1980s, the United Auto Workers (UAW) was a very responsible participant in the renaissance. Its prime representative, Don Ephlin, was a "symbol of what can be." Today, people at Ford say relationships with the union were "never better." Management and the UAW work together in a sustaining relationship that is like nothing seen before. It's been a very positive development and is critical for sustaining excellence and success.

Part of the cultural change is using the minds as well as the hands of hourly workers. Management listens to suggestions from the blue-collar ranks and takes them seriously. At Ford these days, often you forget who's wearing the suit. Sometimes no one is.

Ford and the Earning Model

It's interesting to see how Ford insiders see their company in relationship to the Earning model. One Ford executive concluded:

> Before the crisis, Entitlement was very strong. Every employee expected a wage increase every year and they weren't shy about insisting on it.
>
> I think we started at 2. Then we had a three-year crisis and went to 9. We began the journey to recovery

with Mr. Ford's speech. That helped get us to 8. Then we made the big changes we needed to and got to 5. We had successful products, we made a lot of money, and the media stories about us said we were the very model of what an American company could be if only they really tried. Of course, we had the advantage of almost going out of business!

Unfortunately, we got to believing the stories and we slid to 4. We got a little too complacent. Then things got tough again and we went to 6. Now, after the last quarter's loss, we're at 7 or 8. We're not at 9 because we've been through this drill before! Right now, 7 is probably a very good place for us to be.

America's Future

As we know, in the years following World War II, governments, schools, universities, and large corporations gave employees essentially absolute job security. The experience of individual employees was so protected from the marketplace, from how well or badly their institution was doing, that the psychological awareness of Earning was lost.

We paid for that, painfully. Our organizations ended up with bloated and inflexible costs and with too many entitled people who, even if they were busy, were not productive. Then the economic barometer shifted, and the stranglehold of competition forced us to make changes.

In the new paradigm, the only way people should be able to get more is to produce more. The only way the nation or an organization can afford increased wages and remain competitive in an international market is for productivity to rise. While productivity has risen an annual 4.1 percent since 1979 in manufacturing, in the service and other nonmanufacturing sectors, where 80 percent of all workers are now employed, productivity grew at less than 0.2 percent a year over the same time period. Unless productivity increases significantly, our standard of living won't rise much. It could even fall. Therefore, in every sector of the economy, but especially in the nonmanufacturing sectors, productivity must rise significantly and swiftly.

We are on the right track. We are witnessing enormous changes in U.S. corporations. Management is shrinking because companies can no longer afford hordes of middle managers who crunch numbers and write reports. Management is also simplifying. Because it is clear that the fat belly of middle management slowed decision making, organizations are reducing the levels of management. It is a very fundamental change. It is a movement away from a hierarchical organization and a vertical distribution of power to a more horizontal organization.

In order to make that work, accountability will have to be direct and specified. But that is easily achievable because horizontal organizations tend to work and solve problems using small, autonomous business units. These small units are held responsible and directly accountable for real results. It's easier for accountability to be assigned, for goals to be defined, and for progress to be measured in small groups.

In the long run, if this change is deliberately managed, it will turn out to be very good news indeed. More people will have the opportunity to be leaders because every team needs a leader. Rather than a progression of promotions, most people will have a series of moments in the sun. Periodically, they will do special assignments, and lead project teams and ad hoc committees. Within successful groups, there will be both a hierarchy of responsibility—someone still has to be the boss—and genuine team interactions between people who are essentially peers.

In a more horizontal structure, where people are peers, everyone is presumed capable of participating and all are compelled to participate by peer pressure. Instead of just looking *up* to see what the boss wants, everyone is also looking *around* that round table. When people are peers, everyone has the right to pressure others to carry their weight.

In summary, then, the goals are to reduce the layers of management and institutional bureaucracy, to shift toward a more horizontal distribution of power, and to create teams of peers that have direct accountability. The results will be greater personal control and confidence; more initiative, experimentation, and risk taking; and greater productivity.

Pushing power down and making people responsible and accountable will result in organizations that can compete, innovate, and flourish. That is the human base for a bright economic future.

America, go to work!

10

On the Personal Side

The psychologies of Entitlement, Fear, and Earning are not restricted to the marketplace. This chapter explores those attitudes as they affect our personal lives, especially within our families. The nonbusiness issue that comes up most frequently is parents' fear that because they did something terrible in rearing their children, the kids now feel entitled. Less common, but not unusual, people describe their elderly parents as being in Entitlement. It is much rarer that people express concern that a spouse, much less themselves, might be there too.

Many Americans are very upwardly mobile, far more successful than their parents were. But despite the success and the affluence, the great majority of them remain psychologically middle class. Psychologically middle-class people derive their sense of self-esteem and the largest component of their identity from their accomplishments. For them, the development of their capacities for excellence, the honing of their character, has been the result of the struggle to accomplish. Their pride is grounded in achievement.

Most psychologically middle-class parents, at whatever economic level, assume that will also be the route for identity and self-esteem for their children. The great majority, in fact, fear that without individual accomplishment their children will be deprived of esteem, confidence, and identity. They know the worst thing they could do is give their children too much protection.

Among the affluent, psychologically middle class, no family issue provokes more concern than how to provide for children without destroying them. In 1986, billionaire Warren Buffett announced that he wasn't going to leave his three children any money when he died. Why? Because he loved them. Rich people, he explained, and the children of the rich glibly point out the debilitating effects of welfare and food stamps on the people who receive them. But not many rich people make the connection to the reality that they are born with a lifetime supply of welfare and food stamps. The only difference is that their case worker is called a trust officer and their stamps come in the form of stocks and bonds.

One family I know created a family board that is parallel to the board of the family business. Requests for money from the children (who are in their thirties) are reviewed by the family board. Those requests are evaluated with the same kind of hard eye that the business board has.

In another family where the father is an entrepreneur with many businesses, the kids have been told "You will not inherit any business from me, nor will I give you one. I will, however, sell you one. The price will be fair and I will help you, but success or failure will be yours. You will have to deal with the consequences of what you do."

In still another family, there are three children. Each has an enormous trust fund but doesn't know it. When they graduated from college each was told "Get a job and learn what it's all about. When you've had some years under your belt come back and we'll talk about your working for me. But, understand, you're not inheriting these businesses."

Living in Entitlement

Entitled Children

We would all agree that our children are entitled to our love and a basic sense of security or well-being. Certainly I am not suggesting withholding those things from children. Entitlement, as we're using the term in this book, is not the result of parental generosity. It is, instead, the result of not holding people responsible for performance. It develops when there's no punishment when the achievement is well below ability.

Given all we know about the negative effects of Entitlement, why do we ever allow it to develop in our children? The answers are found deep in the human psyche.

Guilt is one very common reason. In the Introduction to this book. I recount the story of the stressed executive whose daughter haughtily informed him that he "owed" her a car because she had turned sixteen. Although he could not afford it, he bought it. Why? Because he felt guilty. He was afraid he'd hurt her in some terrible way because he'd divorced her mother and no longer lived with them. Because the car was too expensive and was a real sacrifice on his part, giving her the car was an important way to show her how very much he loved her. The car was an attempt to undo the injury he was afraid he'd created by leaving her.

When mothers stayed home, mostly it was fathers who felt guilty for ignoring the kids. Today, even if they are not divorced, both parents are usually employed, working hard and for long hours, so the potential for parental guilt is much higher. Parents may seek to gain the affection of their children and demonstrate their love by giving them things, often at a sacrificial cost to themselves.

Sometimes, out of misguided love, parents are too indulgent. They don't require good grades in school or a disciplined pursuit of athletics or a hobby. They say "I don't want my kids to have a hard time like I did. I don't want them to have to work as hard as I did. I want them to have a good time." That's why Entitlement particularly affects the baby-boomers, a generation who grew up in the decades of economic expansion after World War II.

Sometimes we don't judge, criticize, encourage, praise, teach, model, or require performance because we're not interested enough in what the other person is doing. The ironic resault is that their demands often increase. In part, they're saying, "Pay attention to me."

We also create a psychology of Entitlement when we feel pity. When our expectations of people's ability to perform are very low, then we don't require performance. To require performance would be cruel. Very few people are comfortable being cruel, so instead we try to be kind. Sometimes we are too kind.

Entitled Spouses

While entitlement in families most often takes the form of indulging the kids, sometimes it's a spouse who is indulged.

Pat and Gary had been married for almost twenty-eight years when she moved out. While Pat had been unhappy for a long time, her leaving was still an awful blow to Gary, who felt rejected and abandoned. Nonetheless, while they were arranging the divorce settlement, he felt he had to be as generous in the divorce as he had been during the marriage. His self-esteem required that he continue to be indulgent to her. A corporate executive, affluent rather than rich, he had always financed a luxurious life-style that permitted her to remain at home.

They sold their house and divided all their other investments equally. He gave her first choice of all the things that two people accumulate in a lifetime together: the silver, the paintings, the furniture. Against the advice of his friends and his lawyer, despite the large amount of capital she now had, he volunteered to give her $7,000 per month in alimony.

Pat went from one end of the country to the other telling her friends how cheap Gary had been. "For all those years, all those rotten years, I should have gotten more." Treated for years as an indulged consumer, she feels so entitled to his earnings that she is not able to acknowledge his generosity.

Sometimes we don't require that people hold up their end, we don't act mad when they don't act responsibly, and we don't hold them accountable in the same ways as we do others, because we're afraid they'll reject us. That's especially true in the case of our emotional partners. Creating Entitlement in a sexual and emotional partner is understandable, but it is a poor life strategy. There's no gratitude for that sacrifice.

Entitled Adult Children

An old friend recently complained to me about her son. Mark was thirty-two and had never held a full-time job. He lived at home without paying rent. My friend had become very angry at him for not taking more responsibility for himself, but was torn by the fear that if she cut him off, they would both discover something they were trying to deny: Maybe he couldn't take care of himself. So my friend felt very ambivalent: She resented his dependence and was scared to death of requiring him to become independent.

Mark, too, has mixed feelings about their relationship. He feels that she owes him security because she is his mom, but he also resents the control she has over him because she acts like his mother.

He's very glib about why he has the right to live in his mom's home. He has a thousand excuses, most of which blame others, or accidents about why he doesn't have a serious job. Under the slick excuses, there's tension. He may not consciously realize it, but he's afraid that if she pushed him out he wouldn't be able to manage.

Then there is Cecilia, who managed to remain an undergraduate for nine years. She enrolled in all of the math and statistics classes that the University of Massachusetts offered. Semester after semester, year after year, she'd enroll in five courses, drop two, get a B in one, a D in another, and flunk the third. The next semester she'd re-enroll in the course she had failed and the one in which she got a D. She managed to take some courses three or four times.

Her family supported her through all those years. In fact, they never asked anything from her, even though her education took more than one-third of the family's income. Cecilia wasn't required to do anything. She didn't have to contribute any money and she wasn't required to produce grades as a condition of staying in college.

The parents' generosity stemmed from pity. They couldn't put it into words, but they felt she was fragile and vulnerable. They assumed she would fail, in every kind of way, if they stopped supporting her. Therefore, they collaborated with her evasion of the tougher judgments of the marketplace by financing an endless education.

Because Cecilia never held a job for all the years she remained in school, her relationship with her parents remained that of a child. She never experienced herself as their peer, capable of earning a living and creating an independent life for herself, and her parents never learned to respect her.

People who have earned their way, especially under difficult conditions, may love others even when they don't perform, and they may feel compassion for them, but they will not respect them. People with a psychology of Earning require that others have that same attitude as a minimum for respect.

Thus, parents of adult but dependent children are very likely to feel terrible conflict, especially if the parents are in Earning. On the one hand, they know their continued indulgence of dependence and entitlement is bad for their child. On the other hand, and appropriately, they're terribly scared of the consequences of withdrawing their support or requiring performance as a precondition for support.

Mark and Cecilia's parents were convinced their children couldn't deal successfully with adult reality, a reality which assumes you can and will take care of yourself. Once we assume incompetence, we expect failure. And then we get failure. There's a powerful relationship between the level of performance expected and the level of achievement delivered. When we presume incompetence, unwittingly we create incompetence.

Unrealistic Goals

People who are in Entitlement don't know that's where they are. Because they believe they're owed what they get, they don't bother with thanks. Especially if the giver is in Earning, they are extremely exasperating.

Adults in Entitlement are also frequently annoying to others. For example, they tend to have either no ambition or have unrealistically high goals. They can be very frustrating to deal with as they exaggerate their competencies and ignore their actual deficiencies. They talk excitedly about high ambitions and rationalize away the reasons they've never succeeded. Not only are they typically unaware of their attitudes of Entitlement but they often appear to deny their repetitive failures or nonperformance.

Arnold, at age forty-three, has been overly protected all his

life. From nursery school on, his adoring mother has passion-
ately explained away the reasons for his failures. "His kinder-
garten teacher was a frustrated old maid who took it out on the
kids. His college professors were all foreigners and none of
them could speak English. His boss was a flake with a terrible
wife."

On the other hand, she also always assumed that he would
fail. Therefore, she and everyone else who was close to him
were certain that he'd always need support, psychological and
financial. That's why they never challenge him, never dispute
his explanations of failure, and generally tolerate his boastful
assertions.

He set out to become an architect but he never quite made
it. He got the degree after an extra year in school, but he wasn't
able to do the years of apprenticeship training required for a
license because he couldn't stand working for someone else.
Paradoxically (but understandably, because he has no confidence), he insists on being the authority, the boss. Unable to
practice as an architect, he decided to become a developer. He
told everyone thal all the other developers had cookie cutters
for brains; he would create something unique.

In the ten years since he graduated from college he's never
raised any money for any venture and he's never held a job for
more than a year. He has never earned even an average income,
but that doesn't stop him from thinking up new projects. He
appears not to have a clue as to why no one invests in him. He
uses psychological defenses to both blind him to his failures and
to create the feeling that he's a big shot.

He putters his way through life. He's always looks busy, but
he never grapples with what's real. There are no deadlines. He
continually postpones decisions. His goals are big but vague
and there are no timetables. In that way, he avoids assessing a
life that has drifted into middle age.

Now that he's over forty, even his mother acknowledges
something is wrong. All the people who care about him feel
frustrated. They'd like to shake him by the shoulders and yell
"Look at yourself! Grab hold. Get a job. Go to work. Grow up!"
But they don't say anything. They sense his vulnerability. They

continue their support with only occasional outbursts of impatience or anger when their patience has worn thin.

For Arnold, the psychology of Entitlement has now become a defense against the psychology of Fear. As long as his psychological defenses allow him to perceive himself as entitled, and as long as he can avoid realistic assessments, he postpones his awareness than he is scared to death.

When People Are Victims

We are more likely to sustain Entitlement in people when we believe the reasons for it originate from conditions outside of their control. When we see the cause as visited upon someone, then we see that person as a victim. We don't hold victims responsible for their nonperformance, and thus they are exonerated by those who would otherwise require performance. In addition, once the victims accept the idea they're victims, they have a reason for why they should be excused from normal requirements of responsibility.

The earlier in life the idea of victimization begins, and the longer it continues, the greater the chance that a critical phase in development is passed and movement from Entitlement to Earning becomes impossible.

The way we manage our lives, the means by which we survive, the hurdles we overcome, the accomplishments we achieve, the quality of the work we do, and the ways we deal with what is real are how we earn self-esteem.

Changing Old Patterns

Getting to Fear is never the end goal, but sometimes it is a necessary step in the journey to competence and independence. Without the external pressure of the end of support, Mark and Cecilia are extremely unlikely to leave dependence and Entitlement.

In each case, a judgment call must be made. Could the person who is not performing adequately become adequate under different circumstances?

If the answer is "no," the decision may be made to continue

the support. If the answer is "yes," the conditions that foster dependence and entitlement have to be changed: Mark has to leave his mother's house and survive on his own by getting a real job or be hungry. Cecilia needs to learn that her parents will pay for two more semesters of school and none after that.

When we change the conditions that create Entitlement, we know two things will happen: (1) The person with a psychology of Entitlement will not believe conditions are really changed. Those with the power to alter the conditions will have to make the changes very clear more than once. Leaving Entitlement is not accomplished in one stroke. It's not an act, it's a process that won't be straight or smooth. (2) The person (or people) who imposes the changes will be afraid and ambivalent. That's why a clear understanding of why the conditions of Entitlement are being changed is essential. The person must also be prepared for the recipient's increased fear and attempts at greater dependence. The recipient is very likely to also feel resentment and anger.

Living in Fear

Unlike Entitlement, most of the people who are in Fear know it. The levels of emotion they're experiencing are too great to be controlled. If anything, they feel as if the emotions are controlling them. The amount of emotion is palpable. That's why responses in Fear tend to be more extreme, exaggerated, inexplicable, even bizarre, compared with those in Entitlement.

The lack of confidence in Entitlement results in attempts to avoid situations in which a realistic assessment would lower even further the person's low sense of self-esteem. The lack of confidence in Fear leads to efforts to diminish the amount of emotion being experienced and to create a sense of being in control.

Short-Term Fear

Unlike Entitlement, people can be in Fear because of a short-term change in external conditions. We've all had experience with situations that have created acute stress. Then, the realistic and appropriate response is Fear. In an unfortunately common situation today, for example, many people have become fearful about their jobs as their organization:

- Downsizes because of a shrinking market share;
- Flattens its hierarchy to become more participatory;
- Merges with a competitor and ends up with redundant employees;
- Moves manufacturing offshore; or
- Sells divisions.

Where there had previously been Entitlement or Earning, external conditions have created an internal state of Fear. In fact, Fear is the psychological healthy response to these conditions.

While feeling Fear under these conditions is an appropriate response, people differ a lot in terms of how they handle it. More than a matter of style, this tends to be an issue of confidence. Those who have had a psychology of Earning have an advantage because they're confident.

Tom, age fifty, is married to Lydia, an upper-level manager for General Electric. Three years ago he was fired from his job with a huge auto-parts distribution company because he was within six months of being eligible for the pension plan. Tom and Lydia recovered from their shock in short order and filed a lawsuit against the firm. In the face of his dismissal they got energized instead of debilitated. They also won a large settlement.

It took a while, but he got a job with his former employer's biggest competitor. Helping the new company win was an exquisite pleasure. He was a success very quickly and within a year he was slated to become a vice-president. For two years he looked and sounded great. "How are things?" I'd ask him.

"Hard," he'd say. "The whole industry is being squeezed by competition. But we're getting better all the time. I'm really making headway in getting the changes made that we need."

Then, to his shock, his whole department—sixty-seven people—was eliminated.

Today Lydia is beside herself. "Do you know what he does?" she said to me. "He reads all day. He stays home and he reads. He talks about going into business for himself but he doesn't do anything. I keep asking him if he has a business plan for this week. He always says he's going to make one up, but he doesn't. He just sits in his chair. I say to him, 'What would you do if I made $25,000 a year instead of $80,000?' He just says, 'But you make $80,000.'"

She's furious because he looks, to her, as if he doesn't care about getting a job. Because he doesn't have obvious symptoms—he's not crying or having trouble eating—she doesn't see he's suffering from huge amounts of fear and depression. For the moment, he's coping as best as he can.

Before he can put himself back into the marketplace he has to be in a state of less emotion. Age fifty, fired twice in three years, a man whose confidence has been battered, an expert in an industry that's going downhill, he is scared and sad. He can't do much until he's in less emotional turmoil. Until then he's unable to leave his chair and battle the world.

Another common external condition that takes people into Fear is divorce. It's especially likely for women because fewer women than men remarry. And fewer women than men earn enough to create the life-style they had before the divorce.

Ruth married a man who had inherited enough money that he never needed to work. Their major income came from his investments. She worked part-time as a librarian. They always had full-time household help, a magnificent house, and their own tennis court. They also had Entitled children. The children grew up in a universe in which adults catered to the pleasures of children and children were never required to do anything in return.

After many years, the couple divorced. First Ruth experienced loneliness. Then she learned he'd been spending his capital for years; there wasn't much left. Even working full-time, there was no way she could afford the life she once had. The divorce took her into Fear and the kids further into Entitlement.

Her world is a maelstrom of high emotion. She feels fear for herself, anger at her husband, and guilt about the kids.

"What," she asked me, "can I do? The kids manipulate me and I know it. I'm exhausted."

"Sometimes," I said, "it's peace at any price. Seems to me, that's where you are. When you're feeling better you can start picking up the pieces and straighten the kids out. Give yourself time." In a few years, she'll probably be fine.

Long-Term Fear

With time, people who normally coped can be expected to recover from the extreme of emotion. That's not the case when people's psychology of Fear is the result of a chronic state of high anxiety. When there have been high levels of Fear for a long time, reducing it is much more difficult.

Ben, for example, was a reasonably successful print salesman for thirty years. Married, he had three children and had always been actively involved with them. When the children married and moved out of town, he always chatted with them on the phone at least once a week. By the time he retired at fifty-eight, he had five grandchildren whom he adored. He enjoyed traveling and made a point of taking two vacations a year, at least one of which was overseas. He enjoyed his friends and saw them two or three times a week. He liked to cook for friends, he liked to fish, and he loved to read.

By the time he reached seventy, he had become a very different man. He stopped phoning his children and his grandchildren. He no longer traveled. He stopped entertaining. He stopped seeing friends and justified that by criticizing them. "You can see them," he'd tell his wife, "but don't bring them here. I can't stand them."

The process of deterioration took years. The erosion of his personality was so gradual that the changes were subtle. Friends would say "Have you noticed that Ben doesn't seem to want to go out the way he used to? Have you noticed or is it just me?" Most people said, "Oh, he's all right. It's just his way. It's the way he is."

Gradually, the geographic area he was willing to venture out in got smaller and smaller. It was defined by an area he could walk to. After a while, he would only leave his home if his wife was with him. It was only by cajoling him that she got him out at all.

What was going on? Very slowly, Ben, who had lived a normal life, had become phobic and obsessive. Trying to reduce his acute but vague sense of anxiety, he created a tiny and rigid universe. As long as his wife stayed in that universe, his controls controlled her life.

Since the deterioration was so gradual, neither of them realized that his behavior was abnormal. That's why they never sought help in changing it. While she tried for years to get him to do things she knew he'd always loved, she couldn't succeed. She tried logic and reminiscence. They don't work against Fear.

When high levels of Fear have become chronic, they're not amenable to reduction through reason, affection, obligation, or familiarity. Mental health professionals are needed to provide both support and challenge. Without that kind of intervention, there is a good chance the pathological behaviors, which are the evidence of psychological defenses, will get more and more irrational.

Living in Earning

I've hardly ever seen a parent whose kid was in Earning who didn't take credit for it. For myself, I think it's mostly the kids's doing and not the parents. Parents can't push or haul a kid into Earning. What they can do is communicate their high expectations about what they think their child is capable of, express their pleasure when the expectations are met and their disappointment when they're not, create circumstances in which children experience the results of what they do, and foster conditions in which they are responsible for performing.

In my own experience it's not a matter of telling them what to do as much as it is an assumption of competence. Appropriate to their age and abilities, children are held responsible for themselves. Parents facilitate but they don't do for the kids and they don't excuse nonperformance. They *love* unconditionally, but they *like* proportionate to behavior.

Billy, a third-grader, came to visit me recently. I hadn't

seen him for a year. As I expected, he'd grown a lot, but I hadn't expected a big personality change. He'd always been shy and distant. Now he was bubbly, talkative, and forthcoming. I asked his parents what had happened.

He goes to private school, and for the first two years, the school is basically lenient and forgiving. The principal says the kids mature at different rates and much of the bad behavior disappears as the kids grow out of it. He always acted out a lot, he was the class clown, and his grades were terrible.

We were all waiting for him to get his act together, but it wasn't happening. Then just before Christmas last year, when the first semester was almost over, the principal and his teacher called us in for a conference. They said he had until the end of the next term to get his grades up, or they were "sure there were other schools that would be better for him."

Now we took it seriously. We told Billy he had one term to get it together or he would have to leave the school he loved. Then we asked him what he wanted to do. He said he wanted to stay. We asked if he'd work really hard and he said yes. We told him we'd help him. None of us knew what we were in for.

It's one of the hardest things we ever did as a family. First, we had to find out if there were any reasons why he didn't do better. It turned out he has some learning disabilities. They're the kind you grow out of but that doesn't help him now.

We hired a tutor for him, a woman trained in special education. She came over, after school, three times a week, four times a week during the summer. She drilled him over and over until he had it. She gave him techniques for learning and made him practice over and over. And while [his dad] is on the road most of the time, I sit with him after dinner, every night, and we go over his homework. Sometimes we're at it until 10.

Most of the stuff the tutor had him do would help in the long run, but it didn't do much for the immediate present. His father decided they needed a goal for right now and he made it spelling. Billy had a spelling test every week. His father told him, "You are going to get 100 percent on your spelling test every week, starting next week."

"I don't think I can do it," Billy said.

"Oh, yes you can," his parents replied. The three of them focused on spelling. That became the first subject he did in his homework. He studied the words and then his mother tested him every night. When his father called from out of town, he asked how the spelling was going.

The first week, he got the 100 percent. And the week following that he got 100 percent. Spelling was becoming an area of triumph. He looked forward to spelling. Beginning with spelling, he was learning to concentrate and work hard. For the first time, he was earning academic success. Of course, it was terrific.

Every term, in every grade, there was a special spelling test. The words on it were hard for adults. Billy's father told him he was expected to get 100 percent on it, just like all the other spelling tests.

"I can't," Billy said. "No way. Nobody gets all those right."

"*You* will," his father replied, "because you can." He was the only kid in the whole grade who aced that exam. His confidence soared.

Billy's father said to me:

> You know the message we tend to give our kids because we want them to be confident is "You can do it. It's easy. You won't have any trouble with it. And if you don't do it, we'll love you anyhow." The Japanese give their kids a different message. They say "You can do it, but it's going to be hard. You're going to have to work very hard. And don't even think about not doing it. That's not an option."

It isn't easy to require performance just as it isn't easy to require that your children stand on their own; psychologically it is often much easier to protect them, take care of them, do for them, excuse them, and even ignore them. Requiring responsible behavior means you have to be involved in defining what is expected, you have to decide what the parental role should be, you have to evaluate what they do, and you have to deal with your disappointment and their resentment when the evaluation isn't totally positive.

Perhaps most difficult of all, when you insist that your children be responsible for what they do, is that you can't remain the nonjudgmental nurturant and loving parent of infants. After earliest childhood, to a large extent, the parents' role changes into that of a teacher, a guide, a coach; on the one hand, enthusiastic and encouraging, and on the other, demanding and unsentimental.

Many years ago, when I was a divorced single parent, my son dropped out of college. He had decided to pursue a career as an auto mechanic. It was not in my power to make him stay in school. I couldn't say, "Stay in school or else!" because there was no "or else." If he left school he'd earn his own living. If he left school I'd still love him. Besides, if your goal is to make people responsible for themselves, in principle as well as in practice, you can offer an opinion but you cannot tell people what to do. You can however, help them to realize the consequences of a choice they're making.

With difficulty because I adored him, with discipline because I adored him, I said:

> You're going to do what you've already decided. I know you've not been happy in school. On the other hand, I don't think being an auto mechanic is such a great choice. I want you to know what it's really like being an auto mechanic. You cannot move into this house. You have to have your own place that you pay for and you cannot eat more than one meal a week here. You're going to live on what you earn. Give me a hug! Good luck. Now I guess you'd better start by finding a place to live.

It takes hundreds, perhaps thousands of such experiences in the years of growing up, most of them vastly less dramatic than this one, to create a psychology of Earning. The earlier it's achieved, of course, the easier it is to maintain because there's a core of confidence and an expectation of success.

The people with a psychology of Earning have an advantage: They are more likely to succeed, even when initially they fail, because they are adaptive. They are the people who are more likely to learn from error and failure because they perceive what is real and they change course when that's called for.

Where people with a psychology of Entitlement are clustered, the demands for Entitlement increase. Where many people are in the psychology of Fear, it is a short step to panic. When the clustering is of Earning, the synergy leads to the highest levels of energy and purpose.

Having a psychology of Earning and being in circumstances where Earning is considered the ideal enable people to live their life in an endless process of learning and developing. From a psychological point of view, there's nothing better.

11

Questions and Answers

In the past years, I have presented lectures, seminars, and workshops on the concepts of Entitlement and Earning to many of our largest corporations. The format is often rather informal, and questions are common. Although the companies are very different, the questions are remarkably similar. Here are some of the most frequently asked.

Q: Why is it that to move from Entitlement to Earning you have to go into Fear? Isn't that counterproductive?

A: No. It's essential.

When people have been in Entitlement, especially very deep Entitlement, any movement toward a higher level of risk—even if only a tiny bit higher—feels like Fear to them. Out of Entitlement, the only direction you can go is toward Fear. One way to visualize this is to think of the original bell-shaped curve as a three-dimensional figure (see Fig. 11-1).

You need a level of Fear to provide the motivation to change. General Motors, the world's largest corporate bureaucracy, is beginning to change its traditional adversarial relations with at least some of its workers and to emphasize cooperation instead. Where once workers were required to shut up and follow orders, now they're being asked to think. A team of hourly and salaried employees managed to cut the number of parts in the rear doors of Cadillacs and Oldsmobiles from fifty-two to thirty. That reduced the number of stamping dies from ninety-three to thirty-eight, and the

Figure 11-1. The Earning curve model in three dimensions.

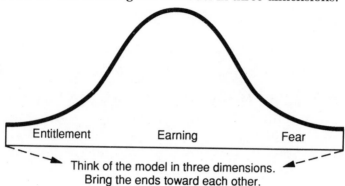

Think of the model in three dimensions.
Bring the ends toward each other.

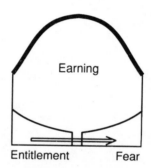

Because any risk is scary, those with a psychology
of Entitlement invariably go into Fear when performance
requirements and accountability are imposed.

number of presses from ninety-three to ten. The company
is saving $52 million a year.

What made the workers want to change? Did they have
a deep inner desire to be empowered? Hardly. The change
is the result of fear. All 310,000 plant workers knew that
40,000 GM workers had been laid off.

People resist change; they also tend to regress, slipping
back to a way of behaving from the past in which they felt
more comfortable. That's why Entitlement continues to
flourish. Thus, when leaders require performance whereas
they didn't before, they are pushing people into Fear. When
they do that, morale plummets: "The leaders of this place

haven't a clue as to what to do. You should have been here in the old days."

This makes it very tough on the leaders. It's hard to sustain the discipline of requiring performance in the light of the bleak mood, especially after the Country Club of Entitlement. But that *must* happen, because the whole drive will be to slide back to Entitlement. Many organizations that were in Entitlement in the 1980s tried to impose requirements of achievement. They instituted all kinds of new systems of evaluation and compensation, but they failed to move into Earning because the leaders lacked the courage to stand fast in the wake of falling morale. The organizations fled back to Entitlement.

The result is that Entitlement is more secure than ever, because when leaders institute new requirements of performance in the future, no one will believe them. It is necessary that requirements for performance be sustained and acted upon so that people learn that the good old days are really gone.

While I was explaining this model in a recent workshop, I noticed one vice-president vigorously nodding his head. "Yes, yes!" he said, "that's what I use!" I asked him what he meant. "I keep pushing and pushing my people, driving them harder and harder, until I know I'm driving them too hard and then I pull back and relieve the tension."

"How do you know where that point is?" I asked.

"I feel it. You just feel it. It's in the air." He paused and then added, "But when you're right in the center, boy, what a high! You're right on your edge, you're pushing as hard as you can. That's when it's exciting. And good."

Q: Will employees resent the corporations as we begin to move them out of Entitlement?

A: Yes.

Q: But don't you run the risk of destroying people's loyalty when you push them out of Entitlement? Surely that's not good for the company.

A: There is no question that finding the balance point can be rather tricky. You don't want to deliberately push people all the way to extreme Fear, to 9, because they become paralyzed. Of course, sometimes external events push them there, but as a deliberate strategy it's foolhardy.

I think that management has to be careful and cautious before they overturn value systems like "The HP Way" or IBM's "Respect for the Individual." These are enormous cultural values that have been critical in creating employee commitment. Pressure for performance, but don't jettison these policies.

Q: Can you have a system that works without horizontal peer pressure?

A: I don't think so.

Q: Why isn't Entitlement a problem in Japan? The Japanese have job security for life—and nothing is more entitled than that—and yet they have the highest productivity in the world.

A: Simple. Japanese firms are famous for pressuring for performance. They have unbelievable peer pressure and also pressure from their hierarchical management.

Interestingly, Susumu Tonegawa, Nobel laureate, has suggested that the qualities that have made Japan an industrial power may be the very ones that make "Japan's science . . . definitely inferior to America's in terms of real creativity." Those qualities include deeply ingrained traditions, acquiescence to authority, strict seniority, little debate, and an immobile work force. They often generate loyalty and teamwork but they don't create far-out, far-ranging breakthroughs. As Tokyo University researcher Zenichiro Honda said "We don't understand in our hearts the joy of taking risks every step of the way."

Q: Where does responsibility lie—with the individual who expects Entitlement, or with the company that allows it?

A: Both.

Q: How long would it take to change a corporation?

A: At least three to five years—unless there's a crisis.

Q: I'm a 5, maybe even a 6, and I'm working in a department where everyone, including the boss, is a 2. How can I get them into Earning?

A: Chances are, you can't. You're not the boss so you don't have the power you need to galvanize energy, require performance, and so on. You'll certainly need a powerful ally to do that.

Of course, you can try. You might begin by talking with the boss and others who are powerful. Your arguments would include the ideas that the department is less productive than it could and should be, and that there's more fun for everyone when people experience the achievement that results from successful risk taking.

But you are already a model of the kind of performance, energy, and risk taking you're advocating and the department has not changed. It has not become more like you.

Without a crisis in which it has become obvious that their ways of operating are ineffective and unproductive, the probability of your changing the culture of the department is small. And, without backing from the boss, it's impossible.

A better strategy would be to leave the department and find an organization where there's a better fit between its culture and your personality.

Q: Why is teamwork counter to a top-down organization?

A: Because in a top-down organization you defer to levels, to someone at a higher level than you, and teams are made of peers.

Q: When people in a work unit have an attitude of Earning, but the boss is still a bureaucrat, how can we protect them? Eventually they'll end up challenging the boss on bureaucratic nonsense. Then what?

A: Some managers still have the mentality that "I know best and you better not question it." When someone does question them, they tend to mutter "I'll get that guy." Until the whole culture begins to change, that person's best strategy is probably to leave. The best thing would be if he or she is really terrific at the job, so that the loss creates a real problem for the manager. Sometimes that's what it takes to shake up people.

Q: I'm the manager in a company that went from a 1 to a 9 practically overnight as a result of a merger. It's taken my department a year and half to get to 7. We still have a couple of supervisors who are back in the old days of Entitlement. Can I fire them, or should I eliminate their jobs?

A: While they are surely irritating to have around, I'd be very careful about firing them. What you would mostly accomplish is to push people further back into Fear. After very high levels of fear, increasing people's sense of fear is not a good idea. The recovery from 9 to 7 is recent and probably fragile. It is more important to further reduce everyone's sense of risk than it is to be rid of two annoying supervisors.

From a strategy perspective, an important question is how other employees perceive the supervisors in question. If others view them as hard workers, if they're held in general affection or respect, if the prevailing attitude toward them is positive, I'd try to change their behavior without resorting to the extreme of pushing them out.

If they are not regarded positively, there are more options, including firing them. That's especially the case if the general view is that they're not pulling their weight under the new and tougher conditions and that management is basically fair. But even then, there's a judgment call about whether firing them would increase the general anxiety level, which would be counterproductive.

I would not recommend eliminating positions as a way to fire people when the department is still recovering from the cynicism, rumor-mongering, and mistrust of high anxiety. Eliminating positions as a mechanism to fire people is an obvious technique and will only increase the mistrust from which the department is recovering. People will say "You can work here for ten years and just like that they get rid of you!"

Q: Why do people think they're in Earning when they really are in Entitlement?

A: Because they're busy.

Q: Making the assessment seems tricky. I'm thinking of some specific individuals. I think I've got them figured out and then one day they look very different.

A: Sometimes people can look as though they alternate where they are on the curve, most frequently between points 2 and 8. But, the points are consistent psychological states or attitudes and you don't have real swift alternations, only apparent ones. Most often people have moved from 2 to 8, and they're trying to cope with the anxiety by insisting they're entitled. It is as though they're trying to deny the change, but the denial is a response to the elevated anxiety level.

Sometimes a person looks like a 2 with peers or the manager and like an 8 with a higher-level boss. That person is probably really a 2, and just very, very careful to stay in the good graces of the superior.

Of course, an extreme set of circumstances, such as being asked to make a presentation to the CEO, could easily take someone into Fear who is normally in Earning. But, in general, people are more consistent in their responses than they are variable.

Q: In terms of where they are on the scale, are people the same in their personal life as they are at work?

A: Generally speaking, yes. I think there's consistency proportionate to the level of confidence. People who have earned confidence in one sector of life are better able (though it's not an absolute given) to intersect in other aspects of life from a base of self-esteem. Similarly, those who have been unable to develop confidence in any major sector of life will, most often, try to avoid situations in which there is real com-

petition and assessment. So people who are fearful at work
are not likely to be courageous in other spheres. Those who
are confident at work are likely to face all their world with
some degree of confidence.

Q: Does the size of the organization determine where that
organization is on the curve?

A: To a degree. It's true that you're far more likely to get Entitlement in larger and richer organizations that don't need
full-out effort from everyone—or didn't used to. Similarly,
it's easier for Entitlement to develop in the bureaucracies of
large institutions, whether corporate, government, health,
or education. And you're more likely to have Fear when
there isn't much of a financial cushion and when there isn't
a legacy of lifetime employment. More frequently that will
characterize smaller organizations, ranging from mom-
and-pop operations to entrepreneurial high-tech start-ups.

And, of course, organizations tend to attract people
whose attitude or relationship to risk is compatible with that
of the organization. We would expect, for instance, that the
old AT&T would have attracted large numbers of people
for whom security was the dominant motive; by the same
token, the start-ups in Silicon Valley are home to many who
thrive on risk and excitement. In that sense, the size of the
organization has some impact on where on the curve people
will tend to be.

The concepts and the Entitlement to Earning model
can be applied to organizations of any size.

Q: Is it possible that different segments of the company are at
different places on the curve?

A: Yes.

Q: I'm not sure that I can apply your model to my own situation. I work in a very small department; there are just four
of us and we're all pretty autonomous. I'm not really responsible for anyone else's contribution.

A: The value of a model is that it helps us understand and make sense out of what we are seeing, so even though you may not be responsible for others, in the sense of being their manager, you can have a fuller understanding of why they work the way they do. You can use that understanding to help create a more effective department, perhaps in informal, even subtle, ways.

For more than twenty years, I was on the faculty of the University of Michigan, and for three years I was also an associate dean there. In my personal office, there were four of us: an assistant dean, an executive secretary, a clerk, and me. While, in a sense, everyone worked for me, in fact we had different jobs and no one really worked for someone else. We were, like your department, basically autonomous.

We were all at least reasonably productive, but our styles were very different and we were at different points on the curve.

The assistant dean was serious, hard-working, competent, thorough, and dependable. He had mastered all the rules and requirements. Whenever there was a sticky question about whether or not a student could graduate, he was the court of last opinion. He most loved using the details he had already learned. He was uncomfortable with abstractions and liked change in small amounts. He didn't like to make big decisions. He was a 4.

The executive secretary was staggeringly competent. She was awesome. She said "My job is to protect you so you can do the things that are important," and that's what she did. She answered my routine correspondence using my words, my style. She typed, she edited, she critiqued, and she suggested. She took care of clients and made sure nothing important ever fell through the cracks. She never had to be told what to do; she was there before I was. She was a 5.

The clerk was a kind, sweet woman for whom there were never any emergencies. She had one pace, slow and steady, and it never varied. She never made mistakes, partly because she never tried anything new. To get her to learn to use computer graphics, we finally had to tell her that if she didn't get sharp on the computer we'd have to let her go.

We knew she could do it. She just had to be shoved into the twentieth century. She was a 3.

And then there was me. In the three years I was in that office, I never did learn the rules of graduation and never intended to learn them. My job, as I saw it, was to be the catalyst for change. Of course, that's how I saw the job because that's my personality. I don't like repetition and detail. I love change and the big picture. I'm a 6.

The model helps me to understand our styles, the sources of our pleasures and frustrations. I don't think either the clerk or the assistant dean would ever be likely to pursue risk by themselves. But where they are on the curve suggests that if some risk taking were required of them and support were provided, the outcome might well be positive. And I think it's really useful to know that the 5 was the secretary and not the boss!

Don't forget that you can also use the model to improve your own performance. For me, it's useful to be aware of a tendency to not have a lot of respect for progress in small increments. I have to pay more attention to those opportunities; in that sense, I have something valuable to learn from the assistant dean.

Q: I can see that how you structure the compensation system would have a powerful influence when you're trying to make changes. Could you summarize how this works at various points on the spectrum?

A: First, when an organization is in Entitlement, it's necessary to use an evaluation and compensation system of significantly different rewards and punishments, of clear winners and losers. In fact, under these systems, winners benefit at the expense of losers and the system creates losers.

Ranking or a forced distribution are ways to achieve this winner/loser structure. Ranking always produces the lowest 5 or 10 percent, and a forced distribution (a bell curve) sets out the percentages of people who are allowed to be outstanding (it's never more than 10 percent) and the percentage who are required to be unsatisfactory (typically

5 to 10 percent). We use systems like these to prod employees out of their complacency.

When the organization (or substantial numbers of its employees) is in Fear, that system of required losers as well as winners, of significantly different punishments and rewards, must be maintained, despite the fall in morale, because it's part of the forced journey from Entitlement to Earning. If the pressure were reduced by eliminating the differentials, the response would be a return to Entitlement.

However, there is one exception. If the level of Fear has remained high long enough so it has become a chronic state instead of a crisis peak, if Fear is no longer being experienced as part of a journey but has become a debilitating and oppressive constant, then it's necessary to decrease the level of anxiety. You don't want major differentials in compensation and you don't want a system that requires some people to be losers. At that point, across-the-board salary increases or merit-pay adjustments are appropriate. Evaluations should not require fine distinctions. Instead, assume most people will work somewhere within a broad band of acceptable performance and use just a few categories of performance.

In an experimental program, Cyanamid no longer uses a recommended distribution. Instead, the great majority of people are designated *G*, for good, a very few people are *E*, for exceptional, and another very small group are *U*, for unacceptable. People in the program are pleased to report they find this system less arbitrary than the previous conventional one.

Now, when the organization is in Earning, you don't want a system that requires there to be losers. Here the goal should always be to have as many winners as possible. Therefore, in Earning, the requirements of performance can be set very high, but there is no arbitrarily set limit on how many people can reach or exceed the targets or goals. IBM's 100 percent club is a model of that. To get into the club, you have to hit 100 percent of your target, but there are no limits on how many people can get in; it works so well than many exceed 100 percent.

In Earning you can end up with people evaluated in a range from unacceptable to outstanding, and that means you can get a range of rewards and punishments, but that's the result of people's performance and not the result of an imposed procedure such as ranking or a required forced distribution of performance appraisals.

In Earning, as in Fear, there should be just a few categories of performance, maybe three. Many possible categories will set people against each other in a purposeless competition. When organizations select and train outstanding people, when they retain only outstanding people, and when those people have a psychology of Earning, the distribution of performance will not and should not resemble a bell curve. It will be skewed to the right, toward excellence.

To summarize, differential rewards have to be used where there is Entitlement. Forced differentials, in the sense that only some can gain them ("If I win, you lose"), should not be used where there's Fear because that increases anxiety. They should not be used in Earning because that is where you want to have many earning success.

Q: Is it possible that the model could be applied to other kinds of problems, aside from the business world? I am especially thinking about the public school system, because of my children, but it seems it could be applied to other general issues as well.

A: Remember what a model does: It simply provides a framework, a perspective, for thinking about issues and, ideally, seeing them in a slightly different way. In that sense, the Earning Curve model becomes a useful tool for analyzing several significant issues of our time.

The school system is a big one, to be sure, mostly because of the effect of tenure systems. I believe it also helps us think about Entitlement programs like union pension funds, about government welfare programs, and even about global economic systems. I think it's not unreasonable, for instance, to characterize certain communist countries as economies that are in Entitlement.

Of course, these issues are enormous and complex, and to really look at them takes far more time than we have here. If the Earning concept contributes toward change within U.S. organizations, the purpose of this book will be fulfilled.

Notes on Sources

The source citations are keyed to the text by page number and a short phrase in boldface type.

Chapter 1

Page

10   **Committee to Allocate Office Space:** Judith M. Bardwick, *The Plateauing Trap*. New York: AMACOM, 1986.

11   **"... while getting ahead":** Nancy Gibbs, "How America Has Run Out of Time," *Time* (April 24, 1989), pp. 58–67. Quotation from page 60.

11   **"... for their children":** "Special Report. Warning: The Standard of Living is Slipping," *Business Week* (April 20, 1987), pp. 48–52.

11   **"... outlook—all bad":** James C. Cooper and Kathleen Madigan, "Business Outlook; Desperately Seeking a Dose of Productivity," *Business Week* (February 19, 1990), p. 27.

12   **security is the customer:** Erroll B. Davis, Jr., president, Wisconsin Power and Light, personal communication, 1989.

12   **"... a deck chair on the *Titanic*":** Daniel Machalaba, "Building Steam. Union Pacific Changes Its Hidebound Ways Under New Chairman," *The Wall Street Journal* (January 18, 1989), pp. 1, 9. Reprinted by permission of *The Wall Street Journal,* © 1989, Dow Jones & Company, Inc. All Rights Reserved Worldwide.

12   **cut from the corporate ranks:** L. M. Applegate, J. I. Cash, Jr., and D. Q. Mills, "Information Technology and Tomorrow's

Manager," *Harvard Business Review* (November–December 1988), pp. 128–136.

12   **as high as 2 million:** J. H. McKerring, "An Assessment of the Role That Outplacement Services Play in Addressing the Negative Psychological Impact Experienced Through Mid-Career Job Loss," unpublished thesis, University of San Francisco, September 1988.

13   **at twice the 1989 rate:** Michael J. Mandel, "This Time, the Downturn Is Dressed in Pinstripes," *Business Week* (October 1, 1990), pp. 130–131.

13   **in the early 1990s:** Ron Zemke, "Putting the SQUEEZE on Middle Managers," *Training* (December 1988), pp. 41–46.

13   **employed 16,735,000 people:** J. Wolf, "Career Plateauing in the Public Service: Baby Boom and Employment Bust," *Public Management Forum* (March/April 1983), pp. 160–165.

14   **despite the strength of our economy:** R. M. Tomasko, *Downsizing.* New York: AMACOM, 1987.

15   **". . . You are Family":** Amanda Bennett, "Broken Bonds," *The Wall Street Journal,* December 8, 1989, p. R21. Reprinted by permission of *The Wall Street Journal,* © 1989, Dow Jones & Company, Inc. All Rights Reserved Worldwide.

Chapter 2

Page

20   **if the employer loses.** John Hoerr, "Needed: A Replacement for the Bargaining Table," *Business Week* (January 9, 1989), pp. 38–39.

21   **30,000 pages of regulations:** Norman R. Augustine, "Defense: A Case of Too Many Cooks," *Fortune* (December 5, 1988), pp. 219–220.

21   **7 pages for pencils:** Howard Banks, ed., "What's Ahead for Business," *Forbes* (February 19, 1990), p. 33.

21   **1,200 pages long:** Julie A. Lopez, "Bucking Tradition," *The Wall Street Journal* (March 15, 1989), pp. 1, 8. Reprintd by permission of *The Wall Street Journal,* © 1989, Dow Jones & Company, Inc. All Rights Reserved Worldwide.

22   **". . . a hole in the wall":** Stratford P. Sherman, "The Mind of

Jack Welch," *Fortune* (March 27, 1989), pp. 39–50. Quotation from p. 46.

Chapter 3

Page

31   **That's my world:** Joshua Hyatt, "The Last Shift," *Inc.* (February 1989), pp. 74–80. Reprinted with permission, *Inc.* Magazine (February 1989). Copyright © 1989, by Goldhirsh Group, Inc., 38 Commercial Wharf, Boston, Mass. 02110.

32   **". . . lose your job tomorrow":** Restaino Baker, Schumann & Co., Marketing Research, "Final Report on Focus Groups" (of a utility company), January 1989.

32   **companies cut their payrolls:** Ronald Henkoff, "Cost Cutting: How to Do It Right," *Fortune* (April 9, 1990), pp. 40–49. AMA surveys 1987–1990 on p. 40. 1990 AMA Survey on downsizing, "Summary of Key Findings," is now available.

32   **maintain profits and markets:** Ron Zemke, "The Ups and Downs of Downsizing," *Training* (November 1990), pp. 27–34.

34   **going on around them:** Ibid.

34   **". . . afraid to take risks":** Henkoff, pp. 40, 41.

34   **rate of 2.5 percent annually:** Sherman, pp. 39–50.

34   **or $2.1 million:** Anne B. Fisher, "The Downside of Downsizing," *Fortune* (May 23, 1988), pp. 42–52. Quotation from p. 42.

34   **deteriorated after the layoffs:** Henkoff, p. 40.

35   **". . . I can trust you":** "When Employees Speak, AT&T Listens," *Focus* (December 15, 1987), pp. 4–7.

36–
37   **back to worrying again:** Fisher, p. 42.

38   **substance of real work:** Abraham Zaleznik, "Real Work," *Harvard Business Review* (January–February 1989), pp. 57–64. Quotation from p. 60.

38   **their own work unit:** Hal Burlingame, HWB Planning Conference, Revision (October 27, 1987).

38   **". . . and cooperation among departments":** Tom Thomas, "Employees Strongly Committed, Unsure About Future," *PG&E Week* (August 14, 1987), pp. 1–3. Quotation from p. 3.

39   **they can't share information:** Walter Kiechel III, "How Important Is Morale, Really?" *Fortune* (February 13, 1989), pp. 121–122.

39   **". . . 'It's mine, all mine' ":** Jacob M. Schlesinger and Paul Ingrassia, "People Power: GM Woos Employees by Listening to Them, Talking of Its 'Team,' " *The Wall Street Journal* (January 12, 1989), pp. 1, 7. Quotation from p. 1. Reprinted by permission of *The Wall Street Journal*, © 1989, Dow Jones & Company, Inc. All Rights Reserved Worldwide.

46   **". . . of his subordinate's endurance":** Peter Nulty, "America's Toughest Bosses," *Fortune* (February 27, 1989), pp. 40–54. Quotation from p. 54.

Chapter 4

Page

53   **good of the whole:** Ted Levitt, "From the Editor; Decisions," *Harvard Business Review,* Reprint 89115.

57   **grit and self-control:** Robert E. Kelley, "In Praise of Followers," *Harvard Business Review* (November–December 1988), pp. 142–148.

57   **". . . it's a competitive necessity":** Stratford P. Sherman, "The Mind of Jack Welch," *Fortune* (March 27, 1989), pp. 39–50. Quotation from p. 46.

57–
58   **rewards people who excel:** William Taylor, "The Business of Innovation: An Interview with Paul Cook," *Harvard Business Review* (March–April 1990), pp. 97–106. Quotation from pp. 99–100.

Chapter 5

Page

60   **". . . of anxiety are attained":** Donald Norfolk, *Executive Stress.* New York: Warner Books, 1989. Quotation from p. 12.

60   **uncertainty) reaches 50 percent:** John W. Atkinson, "Motivational Determinants of Risk Taking Behavior," *Psychological Review,* vol. 64, no. 6, 1957, p. 365.

Chapter 6

Page

81–
82 **". . . and provide greater incentives":** Whitman quoted in Thomas A. Stewart, "CEOs See Clout Shifting," *Fortune* (November 6, 1989), p. 66.

83 **at half the cost:** Ronald Henkoff, "Cost Cutting: How to Do It Right," *Fortune* (April 9, 1990), pp. 40–49.

87 **absentees are swiftly noticed:** Louis Kraar, "Japan's Gung-Ho U.S. Car Plants," *Fortune* (January 30, 1989), pp. 98–108.

88 **the car might be like:** Kim B. Clark and Takahiro Fujimoto, "The Power of Product Integrity," *Harvard Business Review* (November–December 1990), pp. 107–118.

88 **for contribution, not status:** Edward E. Lawler III, "Putting It All Together," unpublished manuscript. 19 pages.

89 **increase productivity became clear:** Nancy J. Perry, "Here Come Richer, Riskier Pay Plans," *Fortune* (December 19, 1988), pp. 50–58.

89–
90 **production and financial goals:** Gilbert Fuchsberg, "Managing," *The Wall Street Journal* (April 30, 1990), p. B1. Reprinted by permission of *The Wall Street Journal*, © 1990, Dow Jones & Company, Inc. All Rights Reserved Worldwide.

90 **100 percent of their salary:** "Here Comes GM's Saturn," *Business Week* (April 9, 1990), p. 59.

90 **". . . a tool to drive results":** Fuchsberg, p. B1.

90 **more responsibility and autonomy:** Alan S. Blinder, "Want to Boost Productivity? Try Giving Workers a Say," *Business Week* (April 17, 1989), p. 10.

91 **relation to company performance:** Graef S. Crystal, "Where's the Risk in CEO's Rewards?" *Fortune* (December 19, 1988), p. 62–66.

93 **General Electric, and Westinghouse:** Henkoff, p. 48.

Chapter 7

Page

99 **". . . what you're going to do":** Brian Dumaine, "The New Turnaround Champs," *Fortune* (July 16, 1990), p. 39.

105   **off to go to school:** Michael Brody, "Helping Workers to Work Smarter," *Fortune* (June 8, 1987), pp. 85–88.

105   **on a shared salary basis:** John Neuman, "What to Know Before Trying Japanese Ideas . . ." *Boardroom Reports* (January 15, 1989), p. 5.

Chapter 8

Page

112   **". . . but never vigorously pursued":** Michael E. Porter, "The Competitive Advantage of Nations," *Harvard Business Review* (March–April, 1990), pp. 73–93. Quotation from p. 74. Reprinted by permission of the *Harvard Business Review*. Copyright © 1990 by the President and Fellows of Harvard College; all rights reserved.

117   **opportunities to learn something:** J. Sterling Livingston, "Pygmalion in Management," *Harvard Business Review* (September–October 1988), pp. 121–130. Shaw quotation from p. 121.

117   **questions from the audience:** "New Organization Will Be Quicker to Respond to Customer Needs, *Update Spotlight* (August 27, 1990), vol. 13, no. 31, special edition of the newsletter of Pacific Bell, p. 3.

121   **Waterman calls "directed autonomy":** Robert H. Waterman, *The Renewal Factor: How the Best Get and Keep the Competitive Edge.* New York: Bantam, 1987.

122   **life will improve dramatically:** Noel Tichy and Ram Charan, "Speed, Simplicity, Self-Confidence: An Interview with Jack Welch," *Harvard Business Review* (September–October 1989), pp. 112–120. Quotation from p. 118.

123   **". . . as responsibility and authority":** Thomas A. Stewart, "New Ways to Exercise Power," *Fortune* (November 6, 1989), pp. 52–64. Quotation from p. 52.

123   **". . . to do things than you are":** Ibid., p. 54.

124   **contributed to the company:** Jay W. Lorsch and Haruo Takagi, "Keeping Managers off the Shelf," *Harvard Business Review* (July–August 1986), pp. 60–65.

125   **a worker named Hwang:** Ira Magaziner and Mark Patinkin, "Fast Heat: How Korea Won the Microwave War," *Harvard*

Business Review (January–February 1989), pp. 83–92. Quotation from p. 90.

126 **"... I do a little tap dance":** Adam Smith, "The Modest Billionaire," *Esquire* (October 1988), pp. 103–108. Quotation from p. 108.

Chapter 9

Page

127–

128 **Japan's was 81 percent:** Howard Banks, "What the Gloom-Mongers Overlook," *Forbes* (October 2, 1989), p. 37, 54.

128 **called a "bureaucratic behemoth":** Pat Baldwin, "Focusing on the Big Picture," *American Way* (July 1, 1989), pp. 40–44. Quotation from p. 40.

128 **that included more layoffs:** Associated Press, "Wall Street Focuses on Woes at Kodak," *The San Diego Union* (July 4, 1989), section D, pp. 1, 2.

129 **to more than 46 percent:** Seth Lubove, "Aim, Focus, and Shoot," *Forbes* (November 26, 1990), p. 67.

129 **"... have to do it all over again":** Associated Press, p. 1.

129 **as a paternalistic caretaker:** Keith H. Hammonds, "A Moment Kodak Wants to Capture," *Business Week* (August 27, 1990), pp. 52–53.

129 **"... that is somewhat paternalistic":** Associated Press, p. 2.

129 **over as chairman and CEO:** Lubove, p. 67.

129 **"... this time they are succeeding":** Hammonds, p. 53.

130 **people are controlling themselves:** Thomas A. Stewart, "New Ways to Exercise Power." *Fortune* (November 6, 1989), pp. 52–64. Quotation from p. 52.

130 **"... problem, and then go away":** William Taylor, "The Gray Area," *Harvard Business Review* (January–February 1989), pp. 178–180. Quotation from p. 180.

131–

132 **IBM's Guiding Principles:** From IBM Managers' Manual, Preface, Index/Page: MM-02.1, Issued 3/16/89.

133 **large organizations take eight to ten:** Jack E. Bowsher, *Educating America.* New York: John Wiley, 1989.

134   **give people a new role:** Michael Beer, Russell A. Eisenstat, and Bert Spector, "Why Change Programs Don't Produce Change," *Harvard Business Review* (November–December 1990), pp. 158–166.

134   **". . . environment in which we do business":** Speech delivered at meeting of Wisconsin Power and Light, Green Lake, Wisconsin, September 1, 1987.

138   **and of better quality:** Charles C. Manx and Henry P. Sims, Jr., *Superleadership*. New York: Prentice-Hall, 1989, p. 179. Reprinted by permission of the publisher, Prentice-Hall Press, a division of Simon & Schuster, New York, New York.

139   **". . . to see things work differently":** Manx and Sims, p. 175. Reprinted by permission of the publisher, Prentice-Hall, a division of Simon & Schuster, New York, New York.

139   **the highly successful Taurus:** Ibid. Reprinted by permission of the publisher, Prentice-Hall, a division of Simon & Schuster, New York, New York.

140   **in the first quarter of 1991:** Joseph B. White, "Big Three Auto Makers' Quarterly Loss Could Total $3 Billion, Analysts Believe," *The Wall Street Journal* (March 4, 1991), p. A4.

140   **·Subaru, Isuzu, and Mazda:** Joseph B. White, Krystal Miller, and Robert L. Simison, "GM and Ford Post First-Quarter Deficits, Are Expected to Be Unprofitable for '91," *The Wall Street Journal* (May 1, 1991), p. A3.

140–
141   **primary cause of the recession:** James C. Cooper and Kathleen Madigan, "A Quick Economic Recovery? Don't Bet the Ranch," *Business Week* (February 25, 1991), p. 27.

141   **they can't get financing:** David Wessel and Paul Duke, Jr., "Greenspan Still Expects Upturn; Car Sales Aren't Liberated by Peace," *The Wall Street Journal* (March 14, 1991), p. A2.

141   **are predicted for 1991:** Henry F. Myers, "An Anemic Recovery May Be Very Healthy," *The Wall Street Journal* (March 11, 1991), p. A1.

141   **Real incomes are declining:** James C. Cooper and Kathleen Madigan, "Empty Pockets Are Still Keeping Recovery on Hold," *Business Week* (March 18, 1991), p. 25.

143   **It could even fall:** Ronald Henkoff, "Make Your Office More Productive," *Fortune,* February 25, 1991, pp. 72–84.

144   **Management is also simplifying:** First discussed in Judith M. Bardwick, "Escaping the Plateauing Trap: Advice for Individuals and Organizations," *New Jersey Bell Journal,* vol. 10, no. 2, Summer 1987, pp. 1–12.

Chapter 10

Page

147   **of stocks and bonds:** Adam Smith, "The Modest Billionaire," Esquire (October 1988), pp. 103–108.

Chapter 11

Page

164   **saving $52 million a year:** Alex Taylor III, "The Tasks Facing General Motors," *Fortune* (March 13, 1989), pp. 52–59.

166   **". . . terms of real creativity":** Stephen K. Yoder, "Japan's Scientists Find Pure Research Suffers Under Rigid Life Style," *The Wall Street Journal* (October 31, 1988), pp. A1, A5. Reprinted by permission of *The Wall Street Journal,* © 1988, Down Jones & Company, Inc. All Rights Reserved Worldwide.

173   **the previous conventional one:** Saul W. Gellerman and William A. Hodgson, "Cyanamid's New Take on Performance Appraisal," *Harvard Business Review* (May–June 1988), pp. 36–41.

Index

[Italic page references refer to figures.]

accountability
  in Earning, 51
  increasing, 79, 82–85, 144
  lack of, 18, 67
adult children, Entitlement and,
  149–151
ambivalence, Entitlement and,
  25–26
American Dream, 7, 11
anxiety
  destructive effects of too little,
    28
  Earning Curve model and, *71*
  vs. Fear, 33n
  increasing productivity using,
    81–94
  motivating with, 58–59
  positive side of, 46–47
  productivity and, 60, *61*
  see also Fear
AT&T, 8, 21, 35, 170

baby boom generation, 8, 11
Bell & Howell, 34
bonuses, 89
Bordon Corporation, 89–90
Bowsher, Jack, 133
bureaucracy, 21–22, 167

career-plateaued employees, 1–
  2, 9–10, 20
CBS network, 36–37
challenges, 116–119
  job satisfaction linked to, 55,
    56, 116
  promoting self-, 118–119
  providing, 79, 80, 85–86
  tolerating mistakes to facili-
    tate, 117–118
Chandler, Colby, 128–129
change
  dynamics of, 133–134
  strategies for making, 72–76
children, Entitlement and, 2–3,
  147–149
Coca-Cola Corporation, 93
Colgate-Palmolive, 123
communications company, Fear
  illustrated in, 42–43
competition
  among employees, 38–39, 54,
    104
  as motivator, 50, 54, 92–93
confidence, 28, 52
  increasing, by publicizing
    achievements, 102
Cook, Paul, 57

covenant of good faith and fair dealing, 19–20
creative tension, 54
customer evaluations, 84
customer satisfaction, 12
Cyanimide Corporation, 173

Defense Department, U.S., 21
denial, Fear and, 36
downsizing, 10, 14, 128
employee outplacement services in time of, 100–101
fear of, 32, 34
self-protection against, 38–39
see also layoffs

Earning Curve model, 4, 60–76
applied to public school system, 174–175
changing position on, 72–76
diagram of, 65
Entitlement, Earning, and Fear components of, 61, 62
at Ford Motor, 142–143
mismatch on, between individuals and organizations, 70–72, 73, 167
nine points of, 62–70
organization's size and place on, 170
productivity related to anxiety and, 60, 61
three dimensions of, 164
as verbal profile, 63–64
Earning, 48–59
benefits of, 52–54
characteristics of, 4, 50–52
creating organization of winners with, 58–59
on Earning Curve, 61, 62, 63, 75

at Industrial Computer Source, 48–50
in Japan, 166
motivation for excellence in, 55–58
moving toward, 72–76, see Entitlement, moving away from; Fear, moving away from
self-delusions about, 169
Earning, maintaining, 110–126
creating conditions for, 115–126
managers as models for, 114–115
strategies for, in individuals, 110–114
Earning, in personal life, 158–162, 169–170
Eastman Kodak Corporation, 13, 128–129
educational opportunities for employees, 104–105, 112
employees
competition among, 38–39, 54, 104
empowering attitudes in, 122
involvement of, at Ford Motor, 138
see also individuals
employment-at-will concept, 10, 19–20
employment contract, 7
betrayal of trust and changes in, 34–35
changing nature of, 14–15, 131–133
empowerment, 119–123
job satisfaction linked to, 55, 56–57
new employee attitudes necessary for, 122

new leader attitudes necessary
for, 122–123
new management attitudes
necessary for, 121–122
respecting many forms of
achievement to create, 119–
120
energy company, Fear at, 41–42
Entitlement, 4, 16–30
in American organizations,
18–19
breaking cycle of, 29–30
characteristics of, in hierarchical organizations, 22–27
costs of, 27–29
defined, 3
on Earning Curve, *61*, 62, *63*,
75
example of, 16–18
origins of, 3, 8–10
resentment at leaving, 165–
166
reversion to, 128, 129
rules, bureaucracy, and hierarchy in, 21–22
security and, 19–21
Entitlement, moving away from,
5, 29–30, 77–94, 167
creating excitement using
stress and, *78*
at Ford Motor, 134–143
pressure combined with support for, 77–78, 79, 80
pressure strategies for productivity and, 81–94
three approaches to, 78–80
Entitlement, in personal life,
146–147
in adult children, 149–151
changing from, 153–154
in children, 2–3, 147–149
in spouses, 149

unrealistic goals and, 151–153
victim role and, 153
entrepreneurial activity, 111,
118
Ephlin, Don, 142
evaluation systems
excessively positive, 64–65
increasing accountability with,
82–85
job security and, 20
excellence
focus on, 111–112, 114
motivation for, 55–58
Exxon Corporation, 13

fairness, enforcing, 106
Fear, 31–47
vs. anxiety, 33n
characteristics of, 4, 35–37
coping techniques of, 37–40
on Earning Curve, *61*, 62, *63–
64*, 75
example of, in three corporations, 40–45
example of individual's, 31–33
manager's task when facing,
45–46
in organizations, 33–35
positive side of, 46–47, 163–
165
Fear, moving away from, 95–109
general approaches to, 96–98
honesty policy for, 95, 132
nine strategies for reducing
pressure and, 98–109
Fear, in personal life, 154–158
long-term, 157–158
short-term, 154–157
federal government layoffs, 13
firing employees
difficulty of, 10, 64
for nonperformance, 92, 168–
169

Ford, Henry, II, 135–136
Ford Motor Company
    excessive Fear at supplier for,
        31–33
    new paradigm development at,
        134–143

General Electric, 22, 34, 122
General Motors, 13, 90, 163–165
global economy, growth of, 11–
    12
goals
    communication of, 106–108
    continual raising of, 93, 112
    unrealistic, in Entitlement,
        151–153
good behavior as coping, 37–38
greed, Entitlement and, 26
guilt, 148

Henkoff, Ronald, 34
Hewlett-Packard Corporation, 13
hierarchy, organizational
    changes in, 144–145
    consequences of, to employees,
        22–27
    countering, with teamwork,
        167
    deemphasizing, to reduce
        Fear, 108–109
    Earning Curve and, 65–66
    empowering employees by
        diminishing, 120–121
    Entitlement and, 21–22
    Fear and solace in, 40
    flattening, to reduce Entitle-
        ment, 86–88
Honda, Zenichiro, 166

IBM Corporation, 27, 130, 173
    statement from, 131–132
incentive pay plans, 89–92

inconsistent behavior, Fear and,
    37
individuals
    anxiety in, and Earning Curve
        model, 71
    communicating concern for,
        100–101
    confidence and problem-
        solving in, 52
    Earning Curve mismatch
        between company and, 70–
        72, 73, 167
    Earning Curve points as seen
        in, 67–69, 70
    educational opportunities for,
        104–105, 112
    example of Fear in, 31–33
    strategies for maintaining
        Earning in, 110, 113–114
    strategies for moving away
        from Entitlement in, 80
    strategies for moving away
        from Fear in, 97–98
Industrial Computer Source,
    Earning at, 48–50
information, reducing anxiety by
    providing, 102–103
innovation, 53, 66

Japan, 32, 140, 160, 166
job satisfaction
    challenge and, 55, 56
    empowerment and, 55, 56–57
    significance and, 55, 57–58
job security
    creating procedures to earn,
        104–106
    Entitlement and, 9, 19–20
    institutionalization of, 20–21
    performance and, 12
Johnsonville Foods, 123, 130

Korea, 125–126

labor unions, relations with, at
    Ford Motor, 142
layoffs, 12–14
    avoiding, 105
    at Eastman Kodak, 128–129
    fear of, 32
leadership
    failure of, in organizations,
        66–67
    new attitudes in, for empower-
        ment, 122–123
    new styles in, in new era, 129–
        131
    reducing anxiety by increasing
        visibility of, 99–100
    see also managers
Lewis, Drew, 12

Magaziner, Ira, 125
management paradigm, new
    America's future and, 143–
        145
    change dynamics and, 133–
        134
    at Eastman Kodak, 128–129
    economic factors and, 127–
        128
    at Ford Motor, 134–143
    leadership styles and, 129–131
    new employment contract
        and, 131–133
managers
    change of, to Earning, 74,
        167–168
    empowerment and new atti-
        tudes of, in, 121–122
    firing of, in Entitlement, 168–
        169
    regaining control in climate of
        Fear, 45–46

tasks of, to maintain Earning,
    110–114
tasks of, to move away from
    Entitlement, 78–80
tasks of, to move away from
    Fear, 96–98
see also leadership
Marine Corps, U.S., motivating
    for success in training pro-
        grams of, 58–59
Mark, Reuben, 123
McClelland, David, 60
meritocracy, creating, 93–94
Michel, Richard, 11
middle managers, 14–15, 33–34
Miskowski, Lee, on changes at
    Ford Motor, 134–143
mission statements, 133
    Ford Motor, 136, 137–138
    IBM Corporation, 131–132
models, 60, 170
    managers as, 114–115
    see also Earning Curve model
Monsanto Corporation, 90
motivation
    competition for, 50, 93–94
    for excellence, through job
        satisfaction factors, 55–58
    Fear and, 46, 163–165
    success, winner psychology
        and, 58–59
    success expectations and, 60

Nissan Corporation, 87–88
nonperformance
    firing for, 92, 168–169
    tolerance of, 9–10

organizations
    bureaucracy/rules in, 21–22
    creating trust in, 101–102

organizations (*continued*)
  Earning Curve and segments
    of, 170–172
  Earning Curve and size of,
    170
  Earning Curve mismatch
    between individuals and,
    70–72, *73*, 167
  Earning Curve points as seen
    in, 64–67, *68*
  Entitlement in, 18–19
  Fear in, 33–35
  hierarchical, *see* (hierarchy,
    organizational)
  institutionalized security in,
    20–21
  loyalty to, 165–166
  strategies for maintaining
    Earning in, 110–113
  strategies for moving away
    from Entitlement in, 79–80
  strategies for moving away
    from Fear in, 96–97
Oryx Corporation, 83
overcontrol syndrome, 42

Pacific Bell Corporation, 117
paradigm, *see* management
  paradigm, new
passivity, Entitlement and, 23–
  25
Patinkin, Mark, 125
pay, plans for incentive, 89–92
peer pressure, 86–88, 166
Pepsi Corporation, 93
performance
  evaluating, 82, 83–84
  in Japan, 166
  job security linked to, 12
  reinforcing, with rewards, 85
Petersen, Donald, 139
pity, 148–149

Poling, Harold "Red," 139
post-World War II era, economic
  boom and growth of Entitlement in, 3, 7–10, 143
power
  new leadership style and, 130
  in Fear, 35–37
pressure
  decreasing anxiety by decreas-
    ing, 98–109
  increasing productivity by
    increasing, 81–94
  peer, 86–88, 166
productivity
  as benefit of Earning, 52
  decline in U.S., 1, 11–12, 143–
    144
  Entitlement and, 28, 29
  Fear and, 34
  related to anxiety, 60, *61*
  strategies for using pressure to
    increase, 81–94
profit sharing, earning and, 49–
  50
prosperity in post-World War II
  era, 7–8
  Entitlement developed from,
    8–10
prudence, encouraging, 112, 114
pseudowork, Entitlement and, 23
psychic gridlock, 41

Raychem Corporation, 57
Rayman, Paula, 11
resentment, Entitlement and,
  25–26
retirement packages, 27
rewards
  conditionality in, 80, 88–92
  differential, 88–92
  incentive pay plans, 89–92

reinforcing performance through, 85
structuring, to create change, 172–174
risk
encouraging taking of, 110–111, 113
Fear and avoidance of, 39–40
gaining confidence by facing, 28
moving toward Earning by using, 72
requiring acceptance of, 85–86
rules, excessive organizational, 21–22

safety, seeking, through risk avoidance, 39–40
school system, Earning Curve model applied to, 174–175
self-challenging, 118
self-esteem, 28, 114
  see also confidence
self-protection as coping method, 38
significance
job, maintaining Earning with, 123–126
job satisfaction linked to task, 55, 57–58
spouses, Entitlement and, 149
Stayer, Ralph, 123, 130
strategies
for implementing incentive pay plans, 90–92
for maintaining Earning, 110–114
for moving away from Entitlement, 78–80
for moving away from Fear, 96–98

pressure, for increased productivity, 81–94
support
to decrease anxiety, 96–98
from executive level, 130–131
with pressure, to create change, 77–80

Taylor, William, 130
teamwork
as benefit of Earning, 53–54
building environment of, 105–106
countering hierarchy with, 167
at Ford Motor, 138, 139
Telnack, Jack, 139–140
tenure, 19, 20
informal organizational, 65
territoriality, Fear and, 38–39
3M Corporation, 111
Tomasko, Robert, 14
Tonegewa, Susumu, 166
Toronto Dominion Bank, 86
toughness, regaining control with, 45–46
trust
creating, 101–102
loss of, 34–35, 45, 168

Union Pacific Railroad, 12
United Auto Workers, 142
U.S. economy in post-World War II era, 7–15
changing employment contract in, 14–15, 131–133
contemporary conditions of, 1, 11–14, 127–128, 140–141
decline of, after 1973, 10–11, 127
development of Entitlement in, 3, 7–10, 143

U.S. economy in post-World War
    II era (*continued*)
  productivity in, 1, 11–12, 143–
    144
  prosperity of, 7–8
utility company, Fear illustrated
    at, 43–45

victim role in personal Entitle-
    ment, 153

Waterman, Robert, 121
Welch, Jack, 22, 57, 122

Whirlpool Corporation, 81
Whitman, David, 81–82
Whitmore, Kay, 129
winning, psychology of, 51
work, evaluating real, 82–83
worry, Fear and, 36–37

Xerox Corporation, 13

Yerkes-Dodson law, 60

Zemke, Ron, 32